SOCIAL POLICY IN AMERICAN SOCIETY

SOCIAL POLICY IN AMERICAN SOCIETY

Robert S. Magill, Ph.D.

University of Wisconsin-Milwaukee

HUMAN SCIENCES PRESS, INC.
72 FIFTH AVENUE
NEW YORK, N.Y. 10011

Printed in the United States of America
987654321

Library of Congress Cataloging in Publication Data

Magill, Robert S.
  Social policy in American society.

  Bibliography: p.
  Includes index.
    1. United States—Social policy.   2. United States—
Social policy—1980–   .   I. Title.
HN57.M264   1983   361.6′1′0973   83-10758
ISBN 0-89885-138-6

To my wife, Peggy, and my parents, Betty and Dick

CONTENTS

PREFACE

The teaching of American social policy has seemed often uneven and disorganized. At present, there is no agreement about whether the major perspective in the teaching of social policy should be historical, descriptive, or analytic. Further, there does not appear to be a commonly accepted base of knowledge and theory considered essential to an understanding of social policy.

In part, this diffuseness exists because social policy is such a new field of study. It was not until 1935 that the federal government sponsored, in any major way, policies to improve the general welfare of people in need. Further, the teaching of social policy has not been important, because American values have not given an important position to social policy. Americans never have been totally comfortable with the idea that all individuals are not completely self-sufficient. Americans never have been totally comfortable with the knowledge that for their physical, economic, and social sustenance and development, some people need help from outside individuals or agencies.

Finally, social policy has not been given scholarly attention appropriate to its importance in society because social policy, perhaps more than any other type of public policy, involves beliefs, opinions, and values. Many people have ideas about how to raise children, what to do with the poor, and how to handle those who break the law. Social policy has been an area where values predominate. The subject is not seen as a field for careful study and analysis. Therefore, although social policy requires a significant investment in terms of money and the time and energy of government officials and of the public in general, social policy is not taught consistently in this country.

Social Policy in American Society presents American social policy from descriptive, historical, and analytic perspectives. It is an effort to bring together, in one place, knowledge from various disciplines, including history, sociology, political science, philosophy, economics, urban affairs, and social welfare, which relates to American social policy.

This book is divided into five major parts. Part 1 defines the field and describes the major aspects of the American social welfare system. The second part describes the relationship of social welfare to the social structure, the political structure, the economic structure, and to major American values. Particular attention is given to the functioning of social policy in a democratic and capitalist society. The third part presents selected aspects of the historical development of social policy which have major importance for contemporary social policy. The following four chapters present a model for policy development and policy analysis. The book concludes with a chapter on the important factors which will contribute to social policy in the future in a capitalistic democracy.

I am indebted to a great number of people who helped me with this project. My students, my teachers, and my colleagues all contributed to my interest, understanding, and excitement with social policy. Mary Ann Riggs, Robin Hauser, and Susan Barlow-Stanis were able to make sense of my writing as they typed the various drafts of the manuscript. They were quick, accurate, and always pleasant to work with.

My wife, Peggy, shared with me this big undertaking. She spent untold hours editing the various drafts of each chapter. She was invaluable in her contributions to the overall organization and approach of the book and to the best and clearest way to present the material. In addition, she provided the support and the conditions that enabled me to complete this project.

Social Policy in American Society is broadly conceived. It grew in part out of a frustration developed from teaching social policy courses during the past decade without one main source for important social policy material. It grew also out of a desire to contribute to identifying the major approaches and content in this important area. I have tried to make *Social Policy in American Society* both accessible and stimulating to teachers and to students. It is hoped that this book will provoke reflection and discussion about the form and the content of the field of social policy.

Milwaukee
December, 1982

Part I

AN INTRODUCTION TO SOCIAL POLICY

Chapter 1

WHAT IS SOCIAL POLICY?

DEFINITIONS OF SOCIAL POLICY

Understanding the nature of social policy begins with form-ing a clear definition. A social policy is a statement of social goals and means in society's efforts to help meet human needs. Martin Rein writes that ". . . social policy . . . is concerned with social purposes."[1] Social purposes are goals for improving people's lives; goals for the poor, the elderly, the very young, the emo-tionally ill, the addicted, and other needy members of society. Social purposes can be distinguished from other goals. For ex-ample, they are not the goals for the military or the space pro-gram.

Social policies are ". . . principles and courses of action . . ."[2] They tend to be broad statements of purpose and general ap-proaches to accomplish the social purpose. Social policies can be distinguished from social programs. Social programs are more specific. Social programs implement social policy. A typical social policy statement could propose, for example, federal help to communities for the purpose of reducing violence in the family. A social policy might recommend creating safe houses for

3

abused spouses and their children. A program proposal to implement this policy would discuss how the safe house was going to be operated, who would be administering and working in the program, and how much specific program components would cost.[3]

Social policy can be distinguished from personal social services also. Personal social services usually are provided by a social worker and can include various kinds of counseling, advocacy, information and referral, and other basic care functions.[4]

Personal social services are a part of social policy. Social policy includes the broad areas of health, education, and welfare. In addition to social workers, lawyers, businesspeople, accountants, doctors, and others implement social policy. A very small proportion of all social policies include personal social services provided by social workers.

Social policy is one aspect of public policy. Public policy includes all of the policies which come from government at all levels. Social policy is the type of public policy which is devoted to social welfare goals.

It is clear that some policies of government have explicit social purposes. For example, all legislation concerning children, the family, juvenile delinquents, and the elderly has social purposes. However, there are other areas of public policy which do not have explicit social purposes but do have important consequences for social policy and the people it serves. Economic policy has a strong impact on social policy. If policy makers decide to decrease inflation by increasing the number of unemployed persons, there will be serious consequences for clients and for the social welfare system. A government decision to reduce federal social welfare expenditures, based on an economic rationale, is going to have serious consequences for social policy. In fact, there is increasing recognition by politicians and theorists that economic policy and social policy are closely related and cannot be considered separately.[5]

Other types of public policy have consequences for social policy. During the 1950s and 1960s, expressways frequently were built through low income communities. Poor communities suffered this disruption because their members were less likely to offer political opposition than were the residents of middle and upper income communities. However, these transportation policies often had the effect of destroying houses that could have been restored, eliminating neighborhoods that could have been preserved, and isolating minority groups by using highways as physical barriers. Clearly, transportation policy, whose major purpose has been to build roads, has had serious consequences for social policy.

Americans are very concerned with energy conservation— the allocation of dwindling energy supplies and the creation of alternative sources. While energy policy is concerned primarily with the production, distribution, and conservation of energy, there are serious consequences for social policy. For example, people on fixed incomes suffer the most when energy costs rise. Social policy must be concerned also with the social purposes and consequences of other policies whose primary focus may be economic or energy related.

In many Western countries, social welfare policies are primarily the responsibility of the government. However, the United States has a long history of nongovernmental activity. When he studied America in 1831, the Frenchman Alexis de Tocqueville observed that Americans tended to form voluntary associations. In Europe, the government would undertake projects to benefit the community and its members.[6] In contrast, American citizens resisted government action and preferred to join with others in voluntary efforts. In the United States, therefore, the private sector also is important in social policy.

In the governmental sector, the policy making process involves the legislative, administrative, and judicial branches of government. Generally, the legislative branch initiates policy proposals. These proposals are studied and debated. Some proposals eventually are passed and sent to the administrative branch of government for action. Laws that are passed by the legislative branch generally are relatively broad statements of goals and methods for implementing these goals. It is left to the administrative branch to develop specific guidelines which interpret how the actions of the legislative branch are to be implemented. The developing of administrative guidelines is a very important and often overlooked aspect of the policy development and implementation process. Often, the individuals who write the guidelines have as much influence over the shape of a social policy as do legislators. Further, administrators and workers who actually implement social policies sometimes change them in the process.

Recently, the judicial branch of government has become more involved in social policy. To a greater extent than before, the courts have ruled on the constitutionality of social policies and, in the process, affected policy. In such areas as public welfare, child welfare, racial integration, education, and corrections, the judicial system has had a major impact on social policy.

Government on all levels participates in making and implementing various types of social policies. Social Security and Veterans' Benefits are major programs which the federal government operates itself. With some exceptions, such as the federal corrections programs and some programs for Native Americans, all of the other social welfare programs are administered partly or completely by state, county, and local governmental units or by private organizations. Usually there is a partnership, with the federal government contributing some monies to the states and/or localities. Often, private agencies receive some governmental funds to supplement the monies they receive from private sources. Therefore, social policy can be made by various institutions and on a number of levels, including the national level, the regional level, the community level, and the organizational level.[7]

SOCIAL POLICY—CHOOSING BETWEEN ALTERNATIVE SOCIAL GOALS AND MEANS

Social policy is concerned with social goals and means. Frequently, however, there are multiple social goals and means, and often they are in conflict. For example, when there is a legitimate difference between the best interests of a child and of the child's parents, whose interests should the policy support? If a choice has to be made, should society support the interests of the parents or the best interests of the child? How should we allocate scarce resources among different groups in need? What percentage should go to the poor, to the aged, to children, and to other groups? Recently, when there have been conflicts between allocating resources for programs for children or for the elderly, the elderly usually have prevailed. The elderly have become more powerful, because they are an increasing proportion of the population, and because they have become politically active.

In developing a social policy for any group, policy makers need to make many choices about what the purposes of the policy should be and how they are to be accomplished. Disagreements are bound to arise. The way in which these conflicts are resolved will have an important effect on the shape of the resulting policy and on how effective and efficient the policy will be. Therefore, central to the development of social policy is the process of choosing between alternative social goals and means.

How are choices made in the area of social policy? Martin Rein concludes that ". . . policy choices are based on beliefs, on reason, on political compromise."[8] Values and beliefs are especially important in the area of social policy, in contrast to other public policies. Their importance arises from the fact that social policy deals with areas in which many people feel that they have expertise. For example, most people feel that they know how to bring up children and what to do with them when they are disobedient. Many people have an opinion about what to do with those on public welfare, or how to treat those who have broken the law. This broadly based assumption of knowledge and competence is not as common in other areas of public policy. Most people do not have opinions about the best way to launch a space ship to Mars or the relative efforts which should be placed on the prevention and the treatment of cancer. Most people would say that experts should make these decisions. However, in the creation and implementing of social policy, values are extremely important.

Political considerations also greatly influence the choices made in the development of social policies.[9] Interest groups try to convince policy makers to increase or expand programs by which their members will gain, through employment opportunities or through benefits. Conversely, interest groups work to weaken or defeat specific social policies when the groups disagree philosophically with the policies or when they feel the costs are too high or believe the change will cause other areas to lose resources. The resulting struggle for the policy makers' votes can be as significant a force in the formation of policy as an objective assessment of which policy would be most effective and efficient.

Finally, in addition to values and politics, research and rationality can be employed to resolve differences between conflicting social policy goals. Unfortunately, research and rationality rarely take precedence over values and politics in resolving conflicts about social policy goals and means. Research and rationality carry too little weight, in part because there is a lack of relevant research in many areas of social policy and in part because values and political considerations are more important to politicians.

Even when empirical studies clearly show that certain types of programs are costly and ineffective, values and politics can prevail over rationality and research. For example, for the past 20 years, the country has been developing job training programs for welfare recipients and for the unemployed. These programs have been costly in terms of money and energy, and they have raised the expectations of the participants. Yet, there is now a large body of evidence which shows that these programs have been only partially effective at best and have been extremely costly when measured in relation to their effectiveness in reducing unemployment.[10] In the future, job training programs for low income persons must be planned more carefully, if they are going to be effective and efficient.

The hope is that as we become more sophisticated in our research methods and engage in more research, conflicts between competing policy goals and means can be resolved more often by rational considerations, than by values and politics.

HUMAN SERVICE WORKERS AND SOCIAL POLICY

Human Service workers are in a unique position to identify problems in the operation of current policies and the need for new policies. Direct service workers come into daily contact with clients who are affected by social problems. By looking for the common problems of different clients, or aggregating, direct service workers can identify needs for new services.

Direct service workers tend to individualize problems by identifying them with particular clients. The process of aggregating the similar problems of dissimiliar clients prompts workers to think in more general terms. For example, suppose that over the period of a month, a worker found that approximately 30 percent of the caseload was comprised of mothers who wanted to work but had to be home for a few hours in the afternoon to be with their elementary school aged children. While the clients all had other different problems, they shared this problem in common. By the process of aggregation, the worker can identify some of the common human problems. From this knowledge, the worker can develop a policy for a limited after–school day care program which could help the mothers, their children, and society.

It used to be possible for human service workers to decide that their main goal was to become expert social caseworkers. Larger issues of policy and administration were left to others. It is now clear that caseworkers, their practice, their agencies, and their clients all are affected by social policy. Further, since caseworkers have direct contact with clients, they are in an excellent position to assess the problems with existing public policies and the need for new policy. All human service workers, then, should have some knowledge of social policy.

SUMMARY

Social policy is concerned with social goals and the programmatic means to implement these goals. Social policy is one type of public policy. Social policy is concerned also with the social consequences of other types of public policy, especially economic policy. Broad statements of social policy goals are implemented by more specific social programs. Personal social services, such as counseling, advocacy, and referral, are a part of social policy.

Social policy is primarily an enterprise of government, although, in the United States, social policy is made and implemented by private social agencies also. Social policy is made and implemented on a variety of levels, including the national level, the state level, the community level, and the organizational level.

Often there is conflict between alternative social goals. Further, there is conflict between alternative ways to implement the goals through social programs. These conflicts are resolved through the value orientations and opinions of decision makers and of their constituencies, through the interaction of interest groups, and through the appeal to research and rational thought. Because social policy deals in an area where many citizens have opinions, it is not unusual for value and political considerations to dominate the decision making process. The reliance on politics and values to resolve social policy conflicts can result in social policies which are expensive and ineffective, and potentially destructive for clients.

Human service workers, based on their experience with clients, are in a unique position to propose and to implement social policy. To be effective, human service workers must develop skill in identifying the common human needs of different clients.

NOTES

1. Martin Rein, *Social Policy: Issues of Choice and Change.* New York: Random House, 1970, p. 9.

2. David Gil, *Unravelling Social Policy: Theory, Analysis, and Political Action Towards Social Equality.* Cambridge: Schenkman Publishing Company, 1973.

3. For a more detailed distinction, see Daniel Patrick Moynihan, Policy vs. Program in the '70's. *The Public Interest,* Summer 1970, pp. 90–100.

4. For a more detailed discussion, see Sheila Kammerman & Alfred Kahn, *Social Services, Policies and Programs in the United States.* Philadelphia, PA: Temple University Press, 1976.

5. Martin Rein, Equality and Social Policy. *Social Service Review*, December 1977, pp. 565–587.

6. Alexis de Tocqueville, *Democracy in America*. Richard D. Heffner, Ed. New York: Mentor Books, 1956.

7. Alfred J. Kahn, *Theory and Practice of Social Planning*. New York: Russell Sage Foundation, 1969, p. 19.

8. Martin Rein, *Ibid.*

9. For a more complete discussion of the job of a legislator, see Lewis A. Dexter, The Job of a Congressman, In Ira Scharhansky (Eds.), *Policy Analysis in Political Science*. Chicago: Markham Publishing Co., 1970, pp. 259–269.

10. See, for example, Charles Garvin, Audrey D. Smith, William J. Reid, *The Work Incentive Experience*. Montclair, NJ: Allanheld, Osmun and Co., Publishers; Sar A. Levitan, Martin Rein, David Warwick, *Work and Welfare Go Together*. Baltimore, Md.: The Johns Hopkins Press, 1972. Mildred Rein, Work in Welfare: Past Failures and Future Strategies. *Social Service Review*, June 1982, pp. 211–229.

Chapter 2

ASPECTS OF SOCIAL POLICY IN INDUSTRIALIZED COUNTRIES

Redistribution: The Major Goal of Social Policy

Social policy is concerned with social goals. These goals can be thought of on different levels of generality. On the broadest level of generality, the famous English social theorist, Richard Titmuss, felt that equality should be the central goal of social policy. Titmuss wrote that in most societies there was a strong resistance against redistribution and that both the private market and government economic policy often worked against the goal of social equality—against the fair distribution of resources. Therefore, the goal of social equality should be central to social policy efforts. Given the institutional resistance towards a more equitable society, Titmuss and others suggest that efforts at redistribution to achieve equality need to be continuing efforts.[1]

The American philosopher John Rawls has supported the goal of equality. Rawls wrote that in society, inequalities develop among individuals in the distribution of income and wealth and in the distribution of citizenship rights such as liberty, opportunity, and power. For Rawls, justice is fairness, and society is seen as a cooperative venture for mutual advantage. In the truly just society, public policies should be evaluated in terms of their effect on the least advantaged individuals in the society. In other words, public policy should strive for social equality.[2]

Consistent with this approach, David Gil has written that the goals of social policy should be to improve

> the overall quality of life in society,
>
> the circumstances of living of individuals and groups, and
>
> the nature of intra-societal human relations.

The overall quality of life and the circumstances of living of individuals and groups relate to the material goods, social comfort, and satisfaction individuals and groups enjoy in a society. Particular attention should be focused on improving the overall quality of life and the circumstances of living of the least advantaged individuals and groups.

The nature of intra-societal human relations encompasses the relationship of individuals and groups to each other and to society. Of special concern in social policy are the relations in society between different and potentially opposing groups, such as the young and the old, the rich and the poor, men and women, and different ethnic and religious groups.

For David Gil, to achieve these ends, certain means, or societal mechanisms, must be changed. These mechanisms of society are

> the development of resources,
>
> the allocation of status, and
>
> the distribution of rights.

In this conception, the development of resources includes societal decisions and courses of action concerning the type, quality, and quantity of all goods and services in the society. To achieve the goals, social policy should work toward a more equitable distribution of goods and services.

Policy issues regarding status allocation are concerned with the degree to which there is equal access for all members of society and the fairness of the criteria for determining access. Social policy should have the effect of eliminating discrimination. Social policy should insure that all members of society, regardless of age, sex, income, race, and ethnicity, have an equal chance to get an education, to find and hold a good job, and to belong to a social club.

Rights distribution refers to the opportunity for individuals and groups to control material and symbolic resources. To what extent is there an equitable distribution of the opportunity for individuals and groups to control the important decisions in life? In other words, is there an equitable distribution of power in the society? Do all members in the society have the same chance to influence policies which will affect them? David Gil feels that social policy should work towards the goal of a more equitable distribution of power.[3]

These goals and mechanisms provide a useful framework for social policy analysis. When a policy is under consideration, it is important to ask whether the policy will have the consequence of promoting a more equitable distribution of goods and services, opportunities, and power. Further, these goals and mechanisms can be used as guideposts when a policy or a program is being developed.

Not all policies strive for or attain the goal of more equality in society. In fact, many existing policies have opposite consequences.

While there is general understanding that there are rich, middle income, and poor persons in American society, most people do not realize how wide the economic inequalities really are. The noted economist Paul Samuelson has written that if one made an income pyramid out of children's blocks, with each layer representing $1,000 worth of income, most of us would be within a yard of the ground. However, the top of the peak, representing the very rich in the society, would be far higher than the Eiffel Tower.[4]

This wide difference in income, relatively unchanged over the past 30 years, can be presented in a different way. Income differences can be shown by arranging the population in terms

Table 1: Percentage Share of Aggregate Income Received by American Families, Ranked by Income of Head, for 1977

Family Income Rank	1977 Percentage Share of Aggregate Income
Top 5 percent	15.7 percent
Top 20 percent	41.5 percent
Top 40 percent	65.7 percent
Top 60 percent	83.2 percent
Bottom 40 percent	16.9 percent
Bottom 20 percent	5.2 percent

of the percentage of the aggregate income which they receive. Table 1 shows the percentage of share of aggregate income received by sections of the population for 1977.[5]

In other words, in 1977, the top 5 percent of all American families received almost 16 percent of the income. The bottom 20 percent of all the families received only 5.2 percent of the income. The top 20 percent of American families received almost half, 41.5 percent, of all the income. The bottom 40 percent of all families received only 16.9 percent of the income. This distribution has remained relatively unchanged over the past 30 years.

In addition to significant differences in the distribution of income by class, there are differences in terms of race. For example, the median income for white families in 1978 was $18,368, while the median income for nonwhite families was only $11,754.[6] While only 12.1 percent of the white families had yearly incomes under $7,000 a year, 29.9 percent, or almost one-third of the nonwhite families, had incomes below $7,000 in 1978. On the other hand, 78.6 percent of the white families had incomes of $15,000 and over, while only 56.7 percent of the nonwhite families had incomes in this range. Table 2 shows white and nonwhite families ranked by their total money income.[7]

Finally, there are significant differences in income based on sex. For example, during the fourth quarter of 1980, the aver-

Table 2: Families Ranked by Total Money Income in Constant (1974) Dollars and by Race of Head of Household for 1978

Total Money Income	1978
(1974 Dollars)	
Percentage Under $6,999	
White Families	12.1 percent
Nonwhite Families	29.9 percent
Percentage $7,000–9,999	
White Families	9.3 percent
Nonwhite Families	13.6 percent
Percentage $10,000 and over	
White Families	78.6 percent
Nonwhite Families	56.7 percent

age weekly earning of men was $335, while the average weekly earning for women was only $211.[8]

Inequality is clearly evident when the combined effects of ethnic group and sex are shown. Table 3 presents median weekly earnings by race and sex for 1980.[9]

Stated in other terms, the distribution of abilities in American society tends to follow a normal, bell shaped curve, whereas the distribution of income among individuals in the United

Table 3: Median Weekly Earnings of Full-Time Wage and Salary Workers by Selected Characteristics, Annual Averages, 1980

Worker Characteristics	Median Weekly Earnings
White	$273
Men	$329
Women	$206
Black	$219
Men	$247
Women	$190
Hispanic	$214
Men	$238
Women	$177

Distribution of income among individuals

Distribution of abilities among individuals

LOWEST   HIGHEST

Figure 1: The Spread of Incomes and the Spread of Abilities in the United States.

States is skewed towards the lower end of the income scale. If income was distributed in relation to abilities, the two curves would be exactly the same.[10]

In all of the comparisons, it is evident that there are significant inequalities in American society in terms of income and race. These inequalities lend support to the contention that equality should be a major social policy goal.

SOCIAL POLICY AS A UNILATERAL TRANSFER

Kenneth Boulding has written that social policy deals with ". . . those aspects of social life that are characterized not so much by exchange in which a *quid* is got for a *quo* as by unilateral transfers that are justified by some appeal to a status or legitimacy, identity, or community."[11]

For Boulding, social policy transactions have a character different from the character of typical economic transactions. Social policy transactions tend to be in the form of a grant or a gift. They are unilateral. In contrast, in marketplace transactions, the consumer usually pays the full cost of the product or service. The buyer and seller are, in this sense, equal.

Most social welfare programs are subsidized. Clients may pay for some of the cost. In most cases, the community, through the United Fund, private contributions, church donations, or government revenue, pays for part or all of the service. In contrast to transactions in the economic area, where something is given for something received, social welfare interactions are mostly activities characterized in part by the grant or the gift. This giving can be in the form of cash, time, effort, satisfaction, blood, or even life itself.

Toba Schwaber Kerson has written that the gift relationship (unilateral transfer) has a long history in social welfare, beginning with the provision of charity to the poor by more wealthy individuals. The gift exchange involves three aspects—giving, receiving, and repaying. The only way in which the exchange can be equal is if all three obligations, giving, receiving, and repaying, are fulfilled. If all three aspects are not fulfilled, there is higher status for the party who has fulfilled his or her obligations and lower status for the party who has not. "Because clients cannot, and indeed often are not allowed to repay social workers, their status in the relationship remains lower."[12] Generally, in social welfare, giving has been downward, from the rich to the poor, from adults to the young, from the learned to the ignorant, and from the powerful to the powerless.

Historically, both goods and services have been provided to clients. More recently, there has been an increase in the provision of nonmaterial goods and services, such as information and referral services, advocacy, and counseling. These nonmaterial goods and services are harder to measure in terms of value, and therefore harder for the recipient to repay.

Further, in addition to dramatizing differences in status, the gift relationship, or unilateral transfer, can act like a self-fulfilling prophesy. A self-fulfilling prophesy is a prediction which comes true because it was made, believed in, and acted upon. The unilateral transfer continues the identity of the giver and the receiver. Gifts reinforce how the giver perceives the receiver, how the giver perceives himself or herself, and how the receiver perceives himself or herself. According to Schwaber, "the gift carries the image of the giver and the giver's image of the receiver."[13]

While the statuses of giver and receiver are likely to be different, the unilateral transfer may impose some obligations upon the recipient. The provision of help to the poor, for example, carries with it obligations the poor must meet to receive that gift. Society expects welfare recipients to conduct themselves in a frugal and law-abiding way and to attempt to find employment. These obligations may be especially strong for the recipient because of the difference in status which the unilateral transfer embodies. It should be pointed out that these expectations of society are at times and for many individuals unrealistic. Some theorists argue that because of these obligations placed upon the client, the unilateral transfer is really a reciprocal exchange.[14]

The inequality inherent in the unilateral transfer is contrary to long-standing values of professional social work. Social workers feel that to be effective, they must create a democratic and participatory relationship with clients. This feeling is an ethical consideration, and in part, a practical one. It is felt that lecturing clients or trying to control them forcibly is ultimately much less effective than involving clients in working with professionals towards their own rehabilitation. Early social work books, such as Mary Richmond's *Social Diagnosis,* published in 1917, emphasized client participation in the treatment process. Professional ethics, as enunciated by the National Association of Social Workers, clearly indicate the importance of democracy and client participation in the worker-client relationship.

Many social welfare professionals make a major and successful effort to overcome the drawbacks of the unilateral transfer. On the level of the worker-client relationship, the unilateral transfer is important because the relationship can be abused by the worker. On the level of social policy, the unilateral transfer characterizes social welfare interactions. It thus can be used as a way to identify social policy as distinct from marketplace transactions.

SOCIAL POLICY AND THE DEMOGRAPHIC BASE

To an extent, social policy responds to changes in the demography of the country. The United States is an industrialized and urban society. Of the total population, only 4 to 4.5 percent work in agriculture. Almost three-fourths of the people live in urban areas, including the cities and their suburbs. The people of the United States have been very mobile. In the past, almost

20 percent of the families have moved every year. There are indications that as housing is getting harder to buy and sell, this trend is slowing somewhat.

The number of people in poverty has increased. In 1981, 31.8 million Americans were below the official poverty line, according to the Census Bureau. This total was an increase in over two million people in poverty in one year.

Because of a decreasing birthrate and advances in science which are keeping people alive longer, the population is getting older. Ten percent of the population is sixty-five and older (compared with 5 percent in 1930). Almost 20 percent, or one-fifth of the total population, is fifty-five years of age and older. This trend is continuing.[15] Partly because of this trend, 25 percent of the federal government's budget in 1980 was for programs for the elderly, especially for medical and retirement programs.[16]

American families are less stable. The divorce rate is climbing. In 1930, the rate of divorce was 1.6 for every 1,000 persons. In 1977, the rate was 5 divorces for every 1,000 persons.[17]

The size of the American household has declined. From 1970 to 1980, the average number of persons per household declined from 3.11 to 2.75, according to the U.S. Census.[18]

The number of single parent families also is rising. During the 1970s, families headed by women increased more than 51 percent. These families had a median income in 1978 of $8,540. This median was just less than half of the median income for all families. However, only 14.6 percent of all families are headed by women. The majority of all families, 82.5 percent, are traditional husband-wife units.

There has been a big increase in the number of persons living alone or with nonrelatives. Such households made up 26.7 percent of the total in 1980, compared with 19.7 percent in 1970.

There also has been a dramatic increase in the percentage of the population that is foreign-born. The percentage was 4.7 in 1970 and grew to 6.2 in 1980. The nation's minority population increased 4.3 percent, to 16.8 percent of the total population, between 1970 and 1980. A dramatic increase, 61 percent, occurred among those who listed themselves as being of Spanish origin. Persons of Spanish origin now make up 6.5 percent of the nation's population. The number of Blacks, the country's largest minority, increased 17 percent during the past 10 years. Blacks now represent 11.7 percent of the population.[19]

In the United States, then, most people live in urban areas. The population is mobile and is experiencing an increasing divorce rate. Two of the most important institutions, the family and the neighborhood, are not as strong as they used to be. To a greater extent than before, women are in the workforce. The entry of women into the workforce has consequences for the family, because many women now spend less time at home and less time taking care of the children and the house. Further, women are more independent economically. This additional independence has increased their options and power in the family and in society. Finally, when jobs are in short supply, women are competing for employment with others, often young male workers or male minority group members.

High mobility and the high divorce rate result in greatly diminished mutual support, affection, and security from the neighborhood and the family. In addition, these primary groups have become less effective in socialization and social control functions. Because of demographic changes, religious, educational, social welfare, and formal social control institutions, such as the police, increasingly are being asked to perform more support, socialization, and social control functions. These functions formerly were primarily the province of the family and the neighborhood. New social policies should take into account the patterns and the problems created by these changes.

As the population gets older, and less able to take care of itself, government social welfare programs are asked to provide more help for the elderly. Consequently, programs for other groups, such as children, are accorded a lower priority.

Finally, it is clear that, at least in terms of income, race, and gender, there is substantial inequality. There are large differences in the income levels when different classes, different races, and the sexes are compared. There are indications that, after some progress during the 1960s, the degree of inequality is now increasing in American society. To what extent there should be redistribution of resources and how much the government should participate, if at all, are some of the major issues facing public policymakers.

SOCIAL WELFARE IN THE UNITED STATES

The federal government in 1979 spent 21.3 percent of the Gross National Product, the sum of all the goods and services produced in the United States. Of all the governmental expenditures, approximately 19 percent are direct federal expenditures by the federal government. The remaining 81 percent is given to states and to local governments.

During 1980, the federal government spent

33.9% for income security programs,

23.1% for national defense,

16.4% for other programs,

11.2% for interest on the national debt,

10.0% for health programs, and

5.4% for educational programs.

To pay for these programs during 1980, the federal government raised

---

45.6% through the individual income tax,

31.0% through social insurance taxes and contributions,

13.8% through corporate income taxes,

5.0% through excise taxes, and

4.6% through other sources[20]

According to Walter Heller, a former chairman of the President's Council of Economic Advisors under Presidents Kennedy and Johnson, government in the United States spends a relatively small percentage of the Gross National Product when compared to our allies. France, Germany, Britain, and the Netherlands, for example, all spend a higher percentage of their Gross National Products on government than does the United States.[21]

Social welfare programs in this country are operated by government and by private agencies. In 1978, almost three-quarters of all expenditures for social welfare were made by the public sector (government). In 1978, federal, state, and local government spent $394.46 billion on social welfare, while the government and private agencies spent $548.86 billion on social welfare.[22]

Using a broad definition of social welfare, the national government directly operates programs for veterans, federal personnel, Native Americans, and violators of federal law. The federal government undertakes research efforts in the areas of health, education, and welfare. The federal government also administers most parts of the Social Security Program, including Old Age, Survivors, and Disability Benefits, Hospital Insurance, and Supplementary Security Income for the aged and the disabled.

The states administer unemployment insurance (apart from special federal programs for veterans, railroad workers, and government employees) and workmen's compensation (apart from special federal programs). The states also administer income maintenance programs, medical care for the needy, education, child care, direct delivery of goods and services, housing programs, personal social services, correctional programs, and food stamp programs. In some states, some of these policies are implemented through county government, and in a few cases, through city government.

On the county and city level, there are social programs in the areas of health, personal social services, housing, community development, and education. Usually these programs receive all or a part of their funding from federal and state sources. Still, they are operated for city, and in some cases, county residents.

On the federal level, the Departments of Health and Human Services, Education, Labor, and Housing and Urban Development administer most social policies. Virtually every federal department operates some social welfare programs. To an extent, there is coordination on the federal level between departments and through the President's Domestic Council and the Office of Management and Budget. In Congress, there are committees concerned with social security, income maintenance, health, education, the work force, and related matters.[23]

Most states have departments of health and social services, with related committees composed of state legislators. Since, in many states, counties still play a role in the delivery of health, mental health, and income maintenance programs, there are county administrators and county legislators as well who become involved in social policy.

There has been a growth in the past 30 years in the number of social workers needed to operate these programs. For example, in 1940, there were 70,000 people employed as social workers. In 1974, there were more than four times that number or 300,000 people employed as social workers. In addition, there were 70,000 social work aides.[24]

The growth can be seen, too, in educational programs preparing students in social work. In 1929, there were about 1,300 full-time students in 25 master's degree programs in the United States and Canada. In 1979, there were 17,397 students working on their master's degrees in social work in 84 schools in the United States and Canada. Further, there were 30,000 full-time undergraduates in social work in 1978.[25] In 1979, the professional social work organization, the National Association of Social Workers, had 79,973 members.[26]

Summary

There are significant inequalities in American society among classes, ethnic groups, and the sexes. As Quentin and Emmy Lou Schenk write in *Welfare, Society, and the Helping Professions*, "There is an unequal distribution of social and economic resources throughout the American Society, and at present the stability of this pattern is more in evidence than is change."[27]

Equality should be the overall goal of social policy. Redistribution of social and economic resources, of status, and of power should be the means to the goal of increased equality. Social policy involves the unilateral transfer. This unilateral transfer is similar to a grant to gift. Therefore, there remains an element of inequality in all social welfare transactions.

To an extent, social policy responds to the demographic base of the society. In the past 80 years, the demographic patterns of the United States have changed markedly. The United States is now an urban, industrialized society. The population has become very mobile. The population is growing older. The divorce rate is climbing, and there are more single parent families. The percentage of the population which is poorer is increasing. These demographic changes indicate the need for new social policies.

Almost three-quarters of all social welfare services have been provided by government. Except for Social Security, Veterans' Benefits, and a few other federally financed and administered programs, most social policies are implemented by state and local governments. Often the federal government provides financial assistance. With the growth of social policy has come an increase in the number of people administering and delivering social policies. Educational programs to prepare students for social work have grown rapidly in number and size during the past 20 years.

NOTES

1. Richard Titmuss, The Role of Redistribution in Social Policy. *Social Security Bulletin,* June 1965, *28,* pp. 14–20; and Martin Rein, Equality and Social Policy. *Social Service Review,* December 1977, *51,* p. 568.

2. John Rawls, *A Theory of Justice.* Cambridge: Belknap Press, 1971.

3. David Gil, *Unravelling Social Policy: Theory, Analysis, and Political Action Towards Social Equality.* Cambridge: Schenkman Publishing Company, 1973.

4. Paul A. Samuelson, *Economics* (9th ed.). New York: McGraw-Hill Book Company, 1973, p. 84.

5. Based on National Association of Social Workers. Table 13. Percentage Share of Aggregate Income, Received by Each Fifth and Top 5 Percent of Families, Ranked by Income and Race of Head, 1947–77. *Statistics on Demographic and Social Welfare Trends.* Washington, D.C., 1980, p. 14.

6. National Association of Social Workers. Table 14. Families Ranked by Total Money Income in Constant (1974) Dollars and By Race of head, 1947–78, *Statistics on Demographic and Social Welfare Trends.* Washington, D.C., 1980, p. 15.

7. Based on National Association of Social Workers, *ibid.,* p. 15.

8. United States Department of Labor, Bureau of Labor Statistics, News. *Earnings of Workers and Their Families: Fourth Quarter of 1980.* Washington, D.C., March 5, 1981.

9. United States Department of Labor, Bureau of Labor Statistics, News adapted from *Table 12; Median Weekly Earnings of Full-Time Wage and Salary Workers by Selected Characteristics, Annual Averages, 1979 and 1980,* Washington, D.C., March 5, 1981.

10. Adapted from Paul Samuelson, *ibid.,* p. 91.

11. Kenneth Boulding, The Boundaries Between Social Policy and Economic Policy. *Social Work,* January 1967, p. 7.

12. Toba Schwaber Kerson, "The Social Work Relationship: A Form of Gift Exchange. *Social Work,* July 1978, p. 326.

13. *Ibid.,* p. 327.

14. Robert Pruger, Social Policy: Unilateral Transfer or Reciprocal Exchange. *Journal of Social Policy,* October 1973, pp. 289–302.

15. Sheila B. Kammerman & Alfred J. Kahn, *Social Services in the United States: Policies and Programs.* Philadelphia: Temple University Press, 1976, pp. 521–554.

16. Robert H. Binstock, A Policy Agenda on Aging for the 1980s. *National Journal Issues Book,* pp. 4–10.

17. National Association of Social Workers. Table 10. Marriage and Divorce Rates, Selected Years, 1900–78. *Statistics on Demographic and Social Welfare Trends.* Washington, D.C., 1980, p. 12.

18. *The Milwaukee Journal,* Households Are Smaller in 1980, May 26, 1981, p. 4.

19. *The Milwaukee Journal,* Percentage of U.S. Non-Whites Grows. 1981, p. 1.

20. U.S. Bureau of the Census, *Statistical Abstract of The United States: 1980* (101st ed.). Washington, D.C., 1980, p. 257.

21. Walter Heller, Economic Rays of Hope. *The Wall Street Journal,* December 31, 1980.

22. Alma W. McMilan & Ann Kallman Bixby, Social Welfare Expenditures, Fiscal Year 1978. *Social Security Bulletin,* May 1980, *43,* pp. 3–17.

23. Kammerman & Kahn, *ibid.*

24. *Ibid.*

25. National Association of Social Workers. Table 50. Full-time Student Enrollment in Master's Degree Programs in Accredited Schools of Social Work and Number of Accredited Schools in the United States and Canada, Selected Years, 1929–79, and Table 51. Students in Accredited Baccalaurate Social Work Programs, By Type of Enrollment, 1974–78. *Statistics on Demographic and Social Welfare Trends,* Washington, D.C., 1980, p. 51.

26. National Association of Social Workers. Table 54. American Association of Social Workers (AASW) Membership, 1921–55; National Association of Social Workers (NASW) Membership, 1956–79. *Statistics on Demographic and Social Trends,* Washington, D.C., 1980, p. 52.

27. Quentin F. Schenk with Emmy Lou Schenk, *Welfare, Society, and the Helping Professions: An Introduction.* New York: Macmillan Publishing Co., Inc. 1981, p. 5.

Part II

THE RELATIONSHIP OF SOCIAL POLICY TO SOCIAL STRUCTURE, VALUES, AND POLITICAL AND ECONOMIC STRUCTURES

Chapter 3

SOCIAL POLICY AND SOCIAL STRUCTURE

INTRODUCTION

Social welfare is concerned with social problems. A problem is social when it affects a large number of people and when there is agreement that something must be done about it. There are thus two aspects of the definition of a social problem—that it is widespread and that there is support for action to ameliorate the condition.[1]

Social problems vary over time. As social and economic conditions change, social problems may become more or less serious. Further, many problems affect a large number of people, but there is not always agreement that something should be done about them. Over time, support for taking action to cope with a given problem may vary. This fluctuation in the desire for social action can be seen readily in the changing attitudes toward poverty, juvenile delinquency, and emotional illness.

There is a relationship between the social problems of a society and the values and institutions in that society. Such problems as crime, addiction, and unemployment are related to social and economic arrangements. For example, the Scandinavian

31

countries virtually have eliminated serious poverty. England and Canada, with their national health insurance, have lower rates of infant mortality than the U.S. A society's social structure and culture are important in determining what problems will occur, where they will occur in terms of factors such as age, ethnicity, and class, and whether there will be social policies to cope with the social problems.

The purpose of this chapter is to examine the function of social welfare in industrial society. In a modern, industrial society, social welfare is an essential institution. Social welfare helps to resolve the conflicts between changing institutions. Social welfare policy also mediates conflicts between generally held societal values and institutions which sometimes do not provide everyone with the means to achieve these values.

Social welfare is especially important in a market economy, because the market does not provide for those who are unable to work. Social welfare policies have economic consequences and, over time, have been especially important in affecting the labor supply.

Social policy has been used as a form of social control also. In this capacity, social policy performs an important function in a modern society.

Finally, social policy provides an expression for people's altruistic impulses. Since before recorded history, people have cooperated with each other. This early social impulse can give meaning and significance to life in a technological society.

SOCIAL POLICY AND INDUSTRIALIZATION

There are certain functions which have to be accomplished in all societies if the societies are to grow and succeed. Human groups survive and prosper to the extent that they successfully organize themselves to provide their members with food, clothing, and shelter, to produce and distribute goods and services, to reproduce and socialize new group members, to maintain internal order and protect themselves from outside attack, and to maintain meaning and motivation.[2]

In relatively simple societies, these systems are related more organically to one another than in complex societies. In simple societies, there is little change in the patterns of life and the institutions that provide structure and continuity. For example, in simple societies, an institution such as religion is closely related to activities in other areas. There may be religious prescriptions about what food to eat, how to bring up children, and how the group should be governed. There are accepted traditions about how the old, the young, and the sick should be taken care of. Typically, group members will help others in times of sickness or emergency through mutual aid and cooperative efforts. In these communities, ownership of the land tends to be communal. The German sociologist Ferdinand Tönnies identified these communities as Gemeinschaft.[3] In these societies, social welfare fulfills a "residual" function.[4]

With industrialization, urbanization, and the division of labor, societies have become larger and more complex. Change has become more rapid. The old organic whole of the preindustrial society has been replaced by less clear and logical relationships among the parts of societies. The values of private property, the profit motive, and individual gain are dominant. Tönnies called these communities Gesellschaft.[5] Different institutions, such as the family, government, religion, and education change, and social needs are left unmet. A major function of social welfare in an industrial society is to help those whose problems have been caused by the complexity and institutional conflict characteristic of industrial society.

For example, the family seems to be doing less of the socialization of children than it once did. The complications and pace of modern life and of the two career family make finding enough good quality time and energy for child rearing very difficult for many parents. Other institutions, such as education and religion, have taken over some of the socialization functions previously performed by the family.

However, the needs of some children still are not met adequately. In a modern society, serving some of the needs of children is one role for social welfare. Social service agencies provide day care centers, institutional care, foster care and adoption services. Other agencies offer after-school recreation programs in settlement houses. The Y's, Boys' Clubs, Scouts and other youth serving organizations offer a range of activities. Social service agencies also provide counseling when families are having difficulties with children.

Another example of a modern social problem associated with Gesellschaft is in the area of unemployment. In prehistoric societies, there was enough work for everyone in basic life-support activities such as hunting, fishing, gathering plants and roots, farming, cooking, and weaving. Those who were ill, or who had other problems, often were taken care of by the group. In a modern society, an individual can be unemployed because the economy does not have an appropriate job. When there is a lack of employment opportunities in the private sector, social welfare policies, mostly through government, can provide unemployed workers money and sometimes training, relocation, and jobs.

In addition, modern societies have conflicts between generally prescribed values and institutions. These conflicts create the need for social policies. In other words, the general values and goals of the society, such as social mobility, are not available to all members of the society. Some members of the society are more mobile than others. Mobility may be the result of hard work or of chance, or of a special advantage which some members of the society enjoy and others do not. As Robert Merton writes, ". . . when a system of cultural values extols, virtually above all else, certain common success goals for the population at large while the social structure rigorously restricts or completely closes access to approved modes of reaching these goals for a considerable part of the population, deviant behavior ensues on a large scale."[6]

In their book, *Delinquency and Opportunity,* Lloyd Ohlin and Richard Cloward build on Merton's theory.[7] They describe how delinquency is caused by the lack of opportunity. All youth strive to "make it" in society, but in some communities, the means to achieve culturally prescribed goals are deficient or lacking. A stable family, a good educational system, a safe community, and social contacts all can contribute to an individual's economic success. When these means are missing, individuals attempt to achieve power and wealth though illegitimate means, such as delinquency and criminal activity.[8] Here there is a conflict between the mobility value of the society on the one hand and institutions on the other hand. Institutions such as the family and the school do not function to enable individuals to achieve equally. Social welfare policies are needed to help prevent and to control the resulting social problems, such as juvenile delinquency.

Equality is a value in society. Our Constitution states that all people should be treated equally. And yet there has been discrimination against some groups, such as ethnic and racial minorities, women, the handicapped, and the emotionally ill. A range of social welfare policies is needed to bridge the gap between the generally prescribed societal values and the implementation of these values through social institutions.

A major reason for social welfare in an industrial society, then, is to mediate conflicts within the social structure of the society. These can be produced between major institutions in the society and between important societal values and institutions. In a changing, complex industrial society, one function of social welfare is to solve social problems that are created because the various parts of the society do not fit together well.

This function has been called by Wilensky and Lebeaux the "institutional" function of social welfare.[9] In complex industrial societies, regardless of their political and economic system, social welfare performs a basic, essential, and needed function. Without the institution of social welfare, a modern society would not be able to exist.

SOCIAL POLICY AND THE MARKET ECONOMY

The institution of social welfare exists in all modern societies regardless of their political or economic organization. Social welfare has a particularly important role in societies which have a private market economy. Richard Titmuss has defined social welfare as "acts of government, undertaken for a variety of political reasons, to provide for a range of needs, material and social, and predominantly dependent needs; what the market does not or cannot satisfy for certain designated sections of the population."[10] This section will discuss the last phrase of this definition ". . . what the market does not or cannot satisfy . . ."[11]

The market economy emerged during the Middle Ages, after feudalism. Under feudalism, the feudal lord held almost all of the political and economic power. There was a rigid class system with little opportunity for personal advancement. The serfs, their houses, the land and crops they farmed, and whatever they made or built were owned by the lord. In turn, the lord ultimately was responsible for all of the serfs. Serfs who were unable to work were taken care of by private charity, usually through the church, by the community, and in some cases by the feudal lord.

With the rise of cities and the breakup of the old feudal arrangements, the laws of supply and demand began to take precedence over the paternalism characteristic of feudal times. Individuals no longer had a guaranteed job, guaranteed food, and a guaranteed home. Under the market system, whether individuals worked depended upon their motivation and whether there was a demand for their labor. No longer did the feudal lord collect and redistribute food. Generally, goods and services were produced and distributed according to marketplace demand.

The rigid class structure was replaced by an economic system which emphasized private gain. It was possible for an individual to make economic and social advances. While this opportunity was advantageous for those who had abilities needed at the time, the idea of private gain resulted in significant social and economic inequalities. This early characteristic of the market system—to create classes based on income and wealth—has continued to the present.

Further, the basic idea of the free market was that the laws of supply and demand, when applied to the production and distribution of goods and services and to the distribution of labor, should proceed without governmental intervention. The laws of supply and demand were seen as basic economic truths. It was felt that government should not make any effort to control or influence supply or demand.[12]

This system may have some utility for those in the work force. However, a pure market system makes no provision for children, the aged, the handicapped, the emotionally ill, and others who, for a number of different reasons, are not taken care of by relatives and are unable to work. For those who are unable to work, or who are paid less than a living wage, the market system, by itself, is unfeeling and brutal.

With the breakup of feudalism, it became clear that any market system had to be supplemented by a series of social welfare policies to provide for those who were temporarily or permanently outside of the market. The alternative of life on the street and starvation was unacceptable both from a humanitarian point of view and in terms of social control. Without work and social welfare provisions, people tend to turn toward crime and/or revolution.

A market economy, then, results in substantial social and economic differentiation. Without outside intervention, some individuals have very few resources, and some have none at all. Social welfare is essential to take care of those who, for whatever reason, cannot successfully compete in a market economy. The alternative of not providing a social welfare support system in a market economy is that those individuals who cannot support themselves will die or become criminals or revolutionaries. None of these alternatives is acceptable. All industrial market societies therefore have some form of social welfare.

At a minimum, social welfare in a market economy provides for the poorest members of the society—those who cannot work. However, as shown in the previous chapter, the market society creates large differences in income and wealth. Since 1935, there has been a general consensus that governmental social policy should have some role in the redistribution of resources from the rich to some of the people with less money. This redistribution is intended to moderate the tendency toward inequality inherent in the market system. However, as Richard Titmuss has shown, there is strong resistance against redistribution. He writes that ". . . social policies are by themselves unable adequately to offset the antiequalitarian forces in the economics of advanced industrial nations."[13]

The role of government in attempting to counteract some of the social and economic inequality inherent in the market system is being challenged in the 1980s by those who feel that the federal government should not be involved with affecting the distribution of resources in society. If the federal government lessens its role in social welfare policy, the inherent trend toward inequality of the market can be expected to increase. The result will be that the rich will get richer, and the poor, and segments of the middle class, will get poorer.

SOCIAL POLICY AND THE LABOR FORCE

Social policies can have an important and direct impact on the size of the labor force. In general, social policies tend to be punitive towards workers when there is a large supply of low-skilled workers who are not attracted by jobs with low pay, low status, and undesirable working conditions. Social policies tend to be supportive to workers who are skilled and who are difficult to replace.

Social policies in the United States have reacted to changes in the size and composition of the labor force. Prior to the 1930s, a large part of the labor force was unskilled. The jobs, such as working in the cotton mills or building the railroads, could be accomplished by immigrants who did not have to speak English. Individuals were replaceable, and immigration insured a large pool of motivated workers. Social policies such as unemployment compensation and disability benefits did not exist in most areas.

Government involvement in programs such as unemployment and disability insurance developed in this country during the 1930s. Policy for sustaining workers developed in part because the labor force was becoming more skilled. Individual workers were harder to replace. New workers often needed costly training programs. Employers benefitted from supportive governmental policies for valued employees temporarily unemployed because of disability or economic conditions.

Today, social policy tends to be supportive of high-skill workers who are hard to replace and punitive towards low-skill workers who are easy to replace. Skilled workers today receive health, retirement, salary, and vacation benefits unknown to workers in the 1900s. On the other hand, individuals on AFDC and General Assistance are constantly forced to work, often at pay rates which are below the minimum wage. They usually have difficult working conditions and few if any benefits.

At times, the government pursues conscious policies designed to cause unemployment in order to increase the size of the labor supply and thereby lower inflation. This occurs because with more people out of work, there is more competition for jobs. Therefore wage demands of employees are reduced. In addition, during difficult economic times, workers tend to save more and be more careful about spending. Thus downward pressure is applied to prices.

Some economists believe that during periods of high unemployment, governments should expand benefits for the unemployed in order to maintain social stability. They argue that even with unemployment insurance and other social programs, the large labor supply will exert downward pressure on wages and prices.[14] Some administrations emphasize the opposite direction by reducing social welfare benefits while increasing unemployment to reduce inflation. The lack of extensive social welfare benefits makes the risk of unemployment more serious and places more downward pressure on wages. As Frances Piven and Richard Cloward write, "conservatives believe that, in an industrial society, aid to the needy reduces business profits by enhancing the bargaining power of the labor forces."[15] Further, "slashing social programs will reinstate the terrors of being without a job."[16]

The risk of this approach, of course, is increased inequality, human suffering, and social disruption. Opponents of this approach argue that human needs must be balanced with economic needs. However, it is clear that there is a link between social policy and efforts to control the size of the low skilled labor force.

SOCIAL POLICY AND SOCIAL CONTROL

Another role for social welfare policy in a modern society is the role of social control. Some individuals are destructive to society and its institutions. To protect society, some individuals must be removed partially and some totally from society. The need to protect society applies particularly in relation to some juvenile and adult criminals. Some individuals should be removed from society for their own good. This need to protect the individual applies to some persons who are emotionally ill, some persons who are retarded, some children, and some elderly persons.

The removal of individuals from society by government raises many important issues, such as who should make these decisions, how they should be made, and whose best interest should be served. These are difficult and complicated problems. They involve the areas of civil liberties, values, law, and theory and knowledge about individual and group behavior.

While we tend to believe that social policies always are developed for the good of recipients, governments can use social policies as an instrument of political control. In some countries, for example, political dissidents are punished by being labeled emotionally unstable and are sent to state mental institutions. Social welfare policies, while they can be used to benefit recipients, can be used by government as a form of political and social control as well.

SOCIAL POLICY AND ALTRUISM

A final reason for social policy in a modern society relates to the basic altruistic and humanitarian impulses of the society. In simpler societies there were cooperative and mutual aid efforts.

SOCIAL POLICY AND STRUCTURE 41

These efforts were basic to human survival and became imbedded in the values and social structure of human social organization. Human beings always have had a need to provide for more than selfish and egotistical desires. Humanitarian efforts, in a technological society, give meaning and purpose to life. As Richard Titmuss writes, "altruism by strangers for strangers was and is an attempt to fill a moral void created by applied science."[17]

SUMMARY

The social problems of a society and the social policies which may be developed in response are related to social structure. Social policies are needed in a modern, industrial society, for many reasons. One is that in a complex, changing social structure, conflicts and gaps develop between major institutions. Conflicts also develop between generally accepted cultural goals, such as equality and social mobility, and institutions which often do not function adequately to help all members of the society to achieve these goals. Social welfare is needed to bridge the gap and to lessen the conflicts which occur in a modern, complex, and constantly changing social structure.

A pure market type of economy is beneficial only to those who work or who have an income. The pure market economy makes no provision for those who do not or cannot work. Further, a market economy tends to produce substantial economic differences in income levels. Social policies are essential in a market economy to provide for those who cannot provide for themselves. Since 1935, it has been felt that the federal government, through its social policies, should attempt to moderate the most extreme social and economic inequalities created by a market economy. This function of government in a market market is being opposed by conservatives in the 1980s.

Since the breakup of feudalism, there always has been a close link between social policy and economic policy, with special emphasis on the condition of the labor force. Social policy has been and is used to force low-skilled workers into jobs. Social policy has been and is used also to protect valued workers through unemployment provisions and disability provisions.

Social policies can be used for social control also. It is generally recognized that some persons are too destructive to themselves or to others and need to be removed totally or partially from society. There are serious and difficult ethical, political, and psychological issues related to this area of social policy. In some authoritarian societies, social welfare policies and services have been used for the purpose of political control.

Finally, social policy in a modern society can spring from humanitarian impulses. When societies reach a certain stage of economic development, they are able to develop formal mechanisms to provide for their less able members. Humanitarian social policies are based in the early mutual aid efforts of preindustrial societies and in later religious teachings. Humanitarian social policies give meaning and value to society.

In simple societies, social welfare was not a separate, formally organized institution. It was practiced by most members of a group. Social welfare was a residual function. In a complex and everchanging technological society, social welfare is a necessary institution. Without social policies, society would not be able to function. For Wilensky and Lebeaux, social welfare services are ". . . normal, 'first line' functions of modern industrial society."[18] There is, of course, constant disagreement about the scope of social welfare policy. There is no disagreement, however, even among its critics, about the need for some social welfare policy in an industrial society.

NOTES

1. Harry Gold & Frank R. Scarpitti (eds.), *Combatting Social Problems: Techniques of Intervention.* New York: Holt, Rinehart and Winston, 1967, p. 2.

2. Alfred J. Kahn, The Function of Social Work in the Modern World. In: Alfred J. Kahn, *Issues in American Social Work*, New York: Columbia University Press, 1959, p. 12.

3. Neil Golbert & Harry Specht, *The Emergence of Social Welfare and Social Work* (2nd ed.). Itasca, Ill.: F.E. Peacock Publishers, Inc., 1981, pp. 18–21.

4. Harold Wilensky & Charles N. Lebeaux, *Industrial Society and Social Welfare*. New York: Russell Sage Foundation, 1958.

5. Neil Gilbert & Harry Specht, *ibid.*

6. Robert H. Merton, Social Structure and Anomie. In *Social Theory and Social Structure*. Glencoe, Ill.: The Free Press, 1957.

7. Lloyd Ohlin & Richard Cloward, *Delinquency and Opportunity.* Glencoe, Ill.: The Free Press, 1960.

8. *Ibid.*

9. Wilensky & Lebeaux, *ibid.*

10. Richard Titmuss, The Role of Redistribution in Social Policy. *Social Security Bulletin,* June 1969, p. 1.

11. *Ibid.*

12. Karl Polanyi, *The Great Transformation*. Boston: Beacon Press, 1944.

13. Martin Rein, Equality, and Social Policy. *Social Service Review*, December 1977, p. 569.

14. W. Joseph Heffernan, *Introduction to Social Welfare Policy: Power, Scarcity, and Common Human Needs*. Itasca, Ill.: F.E. Peacock Publishers Inc., 1979.

15. Francis Fox Piven & Richard Cloward, Keeping Labor Lean and Hungry. *The Nation*, November 7, 1981, pp. 466.

16. *Ibid.,* 467.

17. Richard Titmuss, The Limits of the Welfare State. *The Correspondent*, March–April, 1964, *31*, p. 46.

18. Wilensky & Lebeaux, p. 138.

Chapter 4

SOCIAL POLICY AND VALUES

INTRODUCTION

Along with social organization, economic structure, and political structure, values are especially significant in influencing social policy. This is because the results of existing research do not provide definitive guidelines always for policy development. In the absence of directions suggested by research, values and politics are relied upon by decision makers in social policy. Further, certain values are held so strongly, they often have more influence over social policy formation than even clear research conclusions.

Social policy is an area in which people often have strongly held values. For example, many adults have firm feelings about how to raise children or how to care for the elderly. Many people have definitive ideas about what to do with individuals who do not work or individuals who break the law. Since social policy deals with human problems about which we all have value orientations, these values often are translated into policy.

Other areas of public policy which seem to have a more complicated knowledge base are not affected as much by values as is social policy. For example, few of us would feel competent to choose between alternative approaches to exploring the moon or to organizing medical care in the United States. Few would feel prepared to make a selection from different weapons systems and defense strategies. However, many individuals and groups have strongly held values around issues such as abortion, racial discrimination, the function of the family, the role of women, and expenditures for public welfare. The values underlying these opinions can be and are translated into social welfare policy.

Some of the most powerful American values seem to be in conflict with basic elements of social policy. Individualism, competition, and self-sufficiency conflict with a basic approach of social policy—helping those who are in need. Powerful opinion leaders, such as the conservative economist Milton Friedman, identify as their primary value the freedom of the individual to choose.[1] Friedman and other conservative policymakers oppose almost all infringements on the value of individual freedom. They believe in a minimal role for government and in the importance of the private market. Milton Friedman is opposed to public education, food stamps, and public housing.

Social welfare is an intrusion into the economic marketplace by outside forces. Social welfare can involve centralized, long-range planning in which many people, children, battered women, the elderly, the mentally ill, and others, are taken care of through monies raised by taxes or tax-deductible charitable contributions. Social policies can sometimes infringe on the freedom of the individual. For example, policies which require fair practices in hiring can have negative consequences for those who have benefitted from discrimination. Most people are required to participate in the Social Security System. However, not everyone would contribute if the Social Security System were voluntary. There has been resentment of taxation that supports social welfare programs. Some taxpayers oppose this spending because it limits their economic freedom. Supporters of social welfare policies in Western society, while acknowledging the value of individual freedom, believe that there are collectivistic values, such as helping those in need, which are extremely important. Collectivists feel that the value of individual freedom needs to be balanced by the value of social justice. These examples demonstrate that value conflicts permeate American social policy.

Major American Values

Andrew Dobelstein has identified four central values which have contributed to American social policy.[2] These major values are capitalism, classical liberalism, positivism, and pragmatism.

Capitalism

Under capitalism, the individual has the moral responsibility to pursue wealth in the marketplace. The "work ethic" is important. People who seem able to work but do not are seen as lazy. Social welfare policy consistent with this value would require the able-bodied to work. Welfare should help people to become independent. On the other hand, help should be given to those who clearly cannot work because of some disability.[3]

Classical Liberalism

Classical liberalism is based on the beliefs of individualism and personal freedom. Classical liberalism differs from twentieth century liberalism. Classical liberals believe in a minimal role for government. They want government out of the marketplace and therefore oppose public ownership or regulation of business. Classical liberals believe in participation in voluntary associations as the proper means to accomplish changes which could be undertaken by government. They emphasize the importance of the family and religion.[4] Classical liberals believe that social welfare policy should encourage clients to take care of themselves. Classical liberalism supports limits on governmental intervention and asserts that "self-help is the best help."[5]

Positivism

Positivism states that the laws of biological evolution can be applied to social organization and that society will improve if these laws are allowed to run their course. This approach, also called Social Darwinism, was most powerful during the middle and late 1800s, when social scientists tried to apply to human society the laws of evolution and of demography. Herbert Spencer coined the phrase "survival of the fittest" and glorified the leaders of industry, such as John D. Rockefeller, Andrew Mellon, Henry Ford, and Andrew Carnegie. Spencer and others opposed all aid to the poor because they felt this aid would impede natural social evolution. Herbert Spencer felt that mental institutions, hospitals, and even public education should be abolished. He relied heavily on the work of his predecessor, Charles Darwin. Darwin had concluded "that the natural forces of elimination (of the poor and dependent) served to preserve the best or most 'fit' elements of society. Social welfare institutions, in contrast, functioned to enfeeble the society through their artificial preservation of 'unfit' species."[6]

Spencer's student, William Graham Sumner, embellished this theory. Sumner wrote that the belief in equality was incorrect, since he felt that humans, like animals, were unequal. Sumner emphasized competition and individual advancement, regardless of social consequences.[7] The birth control efforts of Margaret Sanger, the establishment of immigration restrictions in the early 1900s, and the attempt by Adolf Hitler to exterminate a whole race of people, are based on these early theories about human inequality.[8]

Spencer, Sumner, and other Social Darwinists, were extremely powerful in American thought and posed a major threat to the values underlying social welfare policy. The Social Darwinists felt that social reform was not possible and that moral worth was related to material possessions. They were strong supporters of the status quo. In summary, the Social Darwinists emphasized competition and individualism, justified inequality in society, and opposed governmental intervention.[9]

The support for Social Darwinism was challenged by the ideas and attitudes of the progressive era of the late 1800s and early 1900s. Scientists such as Lester Ward showed that excessive competition can prevent the most fit from surviving. For example, flowers or vegetables planted too closely together and overcrowding in underdeveloped nations can result in poor growth and early death. In many situations, without cooperation, nobody survives.

Politically, Social Darwinism lost support as the social consequences of unrestrained capitalism, such as abuse of children and women in the workplace, huge concentrations of wealth and power, and ground, air, and water pollution, became clear. Social policies were pursued as the emerging middle class demanded more security and protection from government.

However, some of the beliefs of the Social Darwinists persist today. For example, many people still believe that those who are different because of emotional illness or the lack of economic resources are somehow less worthy. There often is a stigma attached to those who need financial, emotional, or social help. The basic approach of social welfare, of providing and receiving outside help for those in need, contradicts the value of survival of the fittest. That many people still believe in some or all of the ideas of Social Darwinism limits the development of social policy today.

Pragmatism

Finally, Americans always have had a pragmatic approach to policy. We strongly believe that we should try what works best. If one approach does not work, another should be tried. In part because of this emphasis on means, our social welfare policy often is based on trial and error.[10] Pragmatism has retarded the growth of long-range, centralized planning in social policy. The result is a social welfare system more decentralized and fragmented than welfare systems in many other Western industrial democracies.

Social Mobility—The Central American Value

Of all American values, the most dominant is social mobility. "The dominant value touches almost every part of the lives of most Americans, and becomes the vehicle through which many of the other values are expressed."[11] In American society, social mobility is the yardstick used to measure personal worth. High social mobility is valued. The absence of social mobility is scorned. The valuing of high social mobility explains the dislike for welfare recipients who appear to be failing at living according to this central American value. Further, some of the negative values attached to low social mobility also become associated with those who work with the poor, such as human service professionals.[12]

If the poor are blamed for their position in society, then the rich, who appear to be highly mobile, tend to be valued. While the rich are regarded with some jealousy and suspicion, they are respected because of their social mobility. The dominant American value system thus reinforces the stratification system and the existing distribution of resources.[13] The American value system erects formidable barriers to the less powerful social welfare value of social equality.

Value Conflicts Within American Society

While there are some values which are held generally throughout society, such as social mobility, there are other values which are associated with specific social and economic classes and with specific occupations. For example, it has been shown that there are differences in beliefs regarding the distribution of power in society. The differences in belief are related to an individual's status. Poor people and minorities tend to feel that wealthy individuals control the economy and have most of the power. On the other hand, many wealthy individuals feel that everyone has a chance to succeed in the society.[14]

Several studies have shown that working class individuals exhibited more defeatist attitudes and more of a feeling of powerlessness than did upper status individuals.[15] In a classic study, Herbert Hyman concluded that ". . . lower class individuals *as a group* have a value system that reduces the likelihood of individual advancement."[16] These value systems have an effect on behavior that results in a self-fulfilling prophecy. Many lower class individuals do not believe they can better themselves, so they do not try, and therefore they do not succeed.[17]

Concurring with this conclusion, Melvin Kohn writes that "The essence of higher class position is the expectation that one's decisions and actions can be consequential; the essence of lower class position is the belief that one is at the mercy of forces and people beyond one's control and, often, beyond one's understanding."[18]

Many social welfare values can be in opposition to prevailing values. Social workers, for example, believe that all individuals are equal in the right to a good life and a fair chance. Social work values assert that all human beings have basic rights to food, clothing, housing, and medical care. Social workers feel that individuals in difficulty have the right to help and should not have to rely solely on their own resources. Social workers generally believe that the worker-client relationship should be democratic rather than authoritarian. Social workers also believe that human behavior has a purpose. In other words, we act the way we do because of our biological inheritance, our childhood experiences, and our current situation. From this perspective, behavior is not good or bad, moral or immoral. Behavior is the result of many factors, which can be understood and sometimes changed. These values conflict with aspects of capitalism, classical liberalism, positivism, and pragmatism.

From a different perspective, it is possible to isolate dominant and subdominant values in the American value system. Dominant values are held more strongly and by a larger proportion of the population than are subdominant American values. Generally, social welfare values are subdominant. For example, social mobility is a dominant value which is somewhat contrary to the social welfare value of equality. Similarly, self-reliance is a dominant value, while dependency, which is sometimes necessary in social welfare, can be seen as a subdominant value. Because social welfare values generally are subdominant in terms of their power, there may be less support for social policies than for other public policies.[9]

Value differences between social welfare and the general society create problems for the developers of social policy. Value conflicts also can create problems for the individual worker in the implementation of social policy. Often individual workers are in situations where what the client wants and needs and what the profession prescribes are in conflict with what the agency can provide. The tension between client needs, agency programs, and professional values is called role conflict and is a difficult aspect of all of the helping professions. For a variety of reasons, including the dominance of certain American values, social policies may result in provisions which are not totally satisfactory to clients, workers, or professional organizations which monitor and try to improve service. This inability to meet client needs fully can place extra stress on the individual worker, who is at the intersection of these value conflicts.

Value Orientations in Social Welfare Policy—The Individualists and the Collectivists

Historically and currently, it is possible to identify two major value orientations regarding the role of social policy in society. These are the individualist orientation and the collectivist orientation.[20] These two orientations are really opposite ends of a continuum. Many people combine some elements of both the collectivist and individualistic orientation.

Individualists and collectivists differ in their beliefs about

> the source of social problems,
>
> the source of the solution to social problems,
>
> the degree of government participation in social policy,
>
> the level of government participation in social policy, and
>
> the appropriate decision making method in social policy.

Individualists tend to locate the source of a social problem within the individual experiencing the problem. Individualists tend, in William Ryan's words, to "blame the victim."[21] For example, Ryan contends that the poor themselves are blamed for being poor. Society feels that poor people live in a culture of poverty, where the life style differs from others in the society. If individuals, of their own accord, would change their living style, they no longer would be poor.[22] Similarly, the individualistic approach blames alcoholics and drug abusers for their addiction, delinquents for their antisocial activity, and unmarried pregnant women for their pregnancy. Not so long ago in American history, the country blamed Eastern European immigrants for having appearances, languages, and lifestyles that made them different from "mainstream" Americans.

Collectivists feel that the causes of an individual's problems are related to a complex interaction among many factors, including heredity, the family, the community, the school, and the values and institutions in the society. Collectivists feel that just as it is wrong to blame an individual for going to the doctor because he or she broke a leg or caught influenza, so it is not accurate or appropriate to blame someone who is poor, retarded, or mentally ill for his or her problems. Collectivists feel that values and institutions in society have an important role in creating the social problems which become the target of social policies.

To solve social problems, individualists place major responsibility on the individual suffering the problem. For example, individualists feel that the poor should be able to "pull themselves up by their own bootstraps." People who are addicted to some substance, such as alcohol or drugs, should be able, of their own free will, to overcome the addiction.

Collectivists feel that society should help the individual in efforts to change. Most people do not expect the physically ill to recover without the help of a doctor and medicine. Similarly, it is not fair, or effective, to ask an individual to change a very strong behavior pattern and related thinking and feeling without outside help. Collectivists feel that all groups in need, such as children, the elderly, the mentally ill, the poor, and the delinquent should have social welfare programs to help them.

The degree and nature of governmental participation in social policy is one of the major issues that distinguishes those who traditionally have emphasized individual rights and responsibilities from those who have been concerned with society's responsibilities for people with emotional, physical, and social disabilities. Collectivists emphasize society's responsibilities, while individualists emphasize individual rights and responsibilities. Traditionally, collectivists have looked to government in general, and the federal government in particular, as an appropriate vehicle for social policy. Individualists have resisted all but minimal participation by government. This resistance arises from the individualists' feeling that it is generally easier to influence lower levels of government, such as city, county, and state government, than the federal government.

Individualists emphasize the freedom and responsibility of the individual. They fear that too much reliance on government to solve individual problems can weaken freedom, the market form of economy, and individual self-reliance. Individualists feel that both the individual and the society are best served by the relative absence of outside intervention in individual and group problems.

Collectivists favor federal participation in social policy because they feel that most social problems are national problems occurring in all states, and that there should be consistent national social policies to deal with these problems. Further, in the past, interest groups sympathetic to social policy, such as unions and civil rights groups, have been more effective on the national level, while business and rural, and suburban interests less supportive of an expansion of social policy, have been more powerful on the state and regional levels.

When government is needed, individualists generally have favored the delivery of public services by the lowest level of government. Preference is given to municipal government over state government and states' rights before federal involvement.

There are differences in orientation between individualists and collectivists in relation also to the proper way to create public policy in a democracy. In terms of the political structure, individualists usually have preferred a form of pluralism, which is analogous to the economic market. Decisions about who gets what are made in the public arena, often through the competition of powerful individuals and powerful interest groups.In a complicated and diverse society, policy decisions evolve out of the democratic participation of influential individuals and groups. Individualists support the pluralistic approach to public policy decision making. They feel that the common good will emerge as self-interest is pursued in the economy and in public policy.

On the other hand, under a pluralistic philosophy, collectivists point out that there are some groups with important needs who usually do not participate in the policy development process. Generally, the consumers of social welfare services, such as children, battered women, the unemployed, those addicted to drugs, and the mentally ill, have a difficult time affecting social policy when they are competing with more powerful individuals and groups.

Further, when decisions are made on the basis of powerful interest groups, there is a tendency for the interest groups themselves to benefit instead of those whom they are supposed to represent. Large institutions, such as business, labor, and powerful social welfare agencies, often are accused of placing their own survival and growth needs before those of their clients. The pluralistic model of decision making benefits the interest groups that are powerful and that participate in the decision making process.[23] The pluralistic approach to decision making can leave out large groups of unorganized citizens and clients who normally do not participate in the political process and yet often are most in need of services.

Some collectivists feel that social welfare decisions should be made on the basis of expert knowledge, research, rationality, and with client participation. Alternative approaches and their costs, benefits, and consequences should be analyzed rationally. Decisions should be made based on the best interests of clients and include their participation. Critics of the social welfare system frequently blame the pluralistic and interest group nature of the decision making process for the disorganized, inefficient, and sometimes ineffectual delivery of services.

A more rational approach to decision making can have

the consequence of centralizing decision making. A large program, such as Social Security, cannot be run effectively if each branch office in each state develops its own policies. Long-range planning must be done by experts who are able to determine future needs and problems. This centralization of decision making lessens the power and, some assert, the freedom of the individual and makes the growth of big government more likely. Individualists fear this trend as a danger to democracy.[24]

Table 4 summarizes the difference between the individualist and collectivist orientations.

Table 4: Differences Between the Individualist and Collectivist Orientations in Social Welfare

	Individualist	*Collectivist*
Source of social problems	Individual	Combination of factors including heredity, family, community, school, and values and institutions of society
Source of solution for social problems	Individual self-help	Society
Degree of government participation in social policy	Low	High
Preferred level of government participation in social policy	Lowest (local, state)	Highest (federal)
Method of decision making in social policy	Pluralism (interest groups decide)	Research and Rationality (experts and clients decide)

Summary

Values are extremely important in influencing social welfare policy, in part because there often is no clear and irrefutable research evidence to support many social policies. Also, social policy is concerned with problems which are familiar to the general population. Most people have value orientations about various approaches to social welfare policy. These widely held values often are translated into legislation affecting poor people, children, women, delinquents, the mentally ill, and the elderly.

Major American value orientations include support of capitalism, classical liberalism, positivism, and pragmatism. The most dominant American value is social mobility. Often, there is value conflict within a society. Some groups, because of their background and experience, do not hold the major value orientations. Studies have shown that low income persons and minorities do not feel always that the individualistic ethic and a positive, pragmatic approach can be beneficial to them. Middle and upper income people, who have benefited from society, tend to be strong supporters of the major American values such as social mobility.

Currently, there are two major orientations to social policy. These are the collectivist and the individualist orientation. Collectivists and individualists differ in their beliefs about the source of social problems and the solutions to these problems, the degree and level of governmental intervention in social policy, and the appropriate decision making method in social policy. These differences can have powerful effects on social policy. As Marque-Luisa Miringoff writes, ". . . when social problems can be viewed as individually and not societally induced, social reform can be abandoned. Malthus, Darwin, Spenser, Galton, Sanger, Laughlin, Shockley, and others utilized genetic and eugenic rationales to question the desirability and legitimacy of the survival of various groups. In so doing, they challenged the validity of the precepts upon which the social welfare institution is based; protective policies were deemd harmful, their economic support, superfluous. Historic evidence suggests that the idea of elimination, in all its various guises, arises with regularity."[25]

NOTES

1. Milton Friedman, *Capitalism and Freedom*. Chicago: University of Chicago Press, 1972.

2. Andrew W. Dobelstein, *Politics, Economics, and Public Welfare*. Englewood Cliffs, NJ: Prentice-Hall, Inc., 1980, pp. 103–119.

3. *Ibid.*

4. Leopold Tyrmand, The Conservative Ideas in Reagan's Victory. *The Wall Street Journal*, January 20, 1981.

5. Dobelstein, *ibid.*

6. Marque-Luisa Miringoff, The Impact of Population Policy Upon Social Welfare. *Social Service Review*, September, 1980, p. 304.

7. Richard Hofstadter. *Social Darwinism in American Thought*. Boston: Beacon Press, 1944, 1955.

8. *Ibid.*

9. Thomas M. Meenahan & Robert Washington, *Social Policy and Social Welfare: Structure and Applications*. New York: The Free Press, 1980, pp. 90–91.

10. Dobelstein, *ibid.*

11. John E. Tropman, Societal Values and Social Policy: Implications For Social Work. In George Martin, Jr., & Mayer E. Zald (eds.), *Social Welfare in Society*, New York: Columbia University Press, 1981, p. 98.

12. *Ibid.*, pp. 98–102.

13. John Dalphin, *The Persistence of Social Inequality in America*. Cambridge: Schenkman Publishing Co., 1981, pp. 55–62.

14. William H. Form & Joan Rytina, Ideological Beliefs on the Distribution of Power in the United States. *American Sociological Review*, 34, February, pp. 19–31.

15. Marc Fried with E. Fitzgerald, P. Gleicher, C. Hartman & J. Blose, C. Ippolito, E. Bentz, *The World of the Urban Working Class*, Cambridge, Mass.: Harvard University Press, 1973, p. 196.

16. Herbert H. Hyman, The Value Systems of Different Classes: A Social Psychological Contribution to the Analysis of Stratification.

In Herman D. Stein & Richard A. Cloward (eds.), *Social Perspectives on Behavior.* Glencoe, Ill.: The Free Press, 1958, p. 330.

17. *Ibid.*

18. Melvin Kohn, *Class and Conformity: A Study of Values.* Homewood, Ill.: The Dorsey Press, 1969, p. 189.

19. John Tropman, The Constant Crisis: Social Welfare and the American Cultural Structure. *California Sociologist* 1978, 1(1), pp. 59–88.

20. This section is based on Robert Magill. *Community Decision Making for Social Welfare: Federalism, City Government, and the Poor.* New York: Human Services Press, 1979, pp. 19–25.

21. William Ryan, *Blaming the Victim.* New York: Pantheon Books, 1971.

22. *Ibid.*

23. Allen Schick, Systems Politics and Systems Budgeting. *Public Administration Review,* March/April 1969, pp. 137–151.
    pp. 137–151.

24. Magill, *ibid.*

25. Miringoff, *ibid,* pp. 312–313.

SOCIAL POLICY AND POLITICAL AND ECONOMIC STRUCTURES

INTRODUCTION

Social policy is an essential aspect of modern life. Social policy develops to meet needs created by the division of labor and industrialization. All countries which spend more than 5 percent of their Gross National Product on social security are industrialized societies.[1]

Social welfare policy exists in countries which have democratic systems and in those which have authoritarian systems of government. Social policy exists in societies with capitalistic market economies and in those with socialist and communist economies.

A society's values and traditions and its economic, political, cultural, and social institutions all determine the function and scope of social policy. This chapter will discuss how some of the major differences in Western societies have resulted in different approaches to social welfare. A second part of the chapter will analyze the prospects and constraints of social policy in a democracy with a market economy.

As a society becomes industrialized, it has to make a series of decisions about the type of social welfare system that it is going to have. According to Gaston Rimlinger,[2] these policy decisions involve questions about

> Whether social welfare services should be provided to all as a right or to some on the basis of need?
>
> Which citizens should be protected against which risks? Should all citizens be eligible for all programs? Should some citizens be eligible, based on criteria, for some programs?
>
> How responsibility should be divided between the individual and the state for the satisfaction of an individual's social and economic needs?
>
> Who should pay for benefits and how they should be administered.

Based on their traditions, values, and institutions, different societies will answer these questions differently and thus develop different social welfare systems.[3]

UNIVERSAL AND SELECTIVE POLICIES

A basic decision which countries must make in establishing their social policies is which if any of their policies will provide universal coverage. Universal policies include clients as beneficiaries on the basis of a universal status, such as age. As the name implies, universal benefits are for everyone, regardless of need. Social Security is a good example of a universal policy, because almost everyone in the country benefits once he or she reaches a certain age. Age, not need, determines whether a person receives Social Security benefits.

Selective policies are based on need. These policies are available to some people and not to others because of some special need which the recipients have. Policies for poor people, addicted people, and mentally ill people all are examples of selective policies. Most of us will not be poor, or addicted, or mentally ill. Selective policies are for only a proportion of the population because of some special need.

It is possible to make certain generalizations about policies which include clients on the basis of universal criteria. Opposite generalizations can be made about policies which include clients on the basis of selective criteria. Universal policies tend to be more expensive, because they provide benefits to a larger number of persons. Selective policies are not as expensive, because they benefit only those who have a specific need. That is why the insurance part of Social Security, a universal policy, is the single most expensive direct transfer program of the federal government.

Because so many people benefit from universal policies, universal policies tend to be more stable politically than selective policies. If everyone benefits, or expects to benefit from a policy, it will have strong political support. On the other hand, selective policies such as public assistance, which benefit only a small percentage of the population, are more vulnerable politically. There usually are not enough voters who benefit from the policy to furnish selective policies sufficient political support. Politicians always are talking about ways to reduce expenses for public assistance. This continual effort to reduce expenses occurs in part because public assistance is a selective policy.

Universal policies usually are seen as a right of the client. Most people believe that they deserve Social Security or public education. Selective policies tend to have a stigma associated with them. Recipients of selective policies may feel that they are getting something which they do not deserve, or do not deserve totally. While Social Security benefits are seen as a right of all, public assistance is not.

Selective policies tend to provide for a larger element of redistribution than do universal programs. Everyone pays and benefits from universal programs, such as Social Security. Everyone also pays taxes for selective programs, but not everyone benefits from them. Therefore there tends to be a greater degree of redistribution of resources associated with selective policies.

Finally, universal policies tend to promote cooperation and

collective responsibility. Because everyone is covered, the overall quality of the service provided tends to be high. Selective services tend to divide and create barriers to the feeling of community because they treat different citizens differently. There is more of a probability that selective services will be of lower quality. Universal policies are more characteristic of the institutional approach to social welfare, while selective policies are based more on a residual philosophy of social welfare.[4]

Table 5 shows the difference between universal and selective policies.

Table 5: Universal and Selective Policies

Universal	*Selective*
Benefits are provided on basis of universal status, such as age	Benefits are provided on basis of need, which is selective
Policies tend to be more expensive	Policies tend to be less expensive
Policies tend to be politically stable	Policies tend to have less political support
Benefits are seen as a right	Benefits may have a stigma associated with them
Benefits tend to be nonredistributive	Benefits tend to be redistributive
Benefits tend to promote cooperation and collective responsibility	Benefits tend to promote community divisions

Universal and nonuniversal policies really form a continuum. That is to say, there are some policies, such as Social Security Insurance, which are clearly universal. There are other policies, such as social services for juvenile delinquents, which are clearly selective. There are some policies, such as unemployment insurance, which are primarily selective but assume some universal aspects, especially when unemployment rates are high.

Most current social policies in America are selective. Historically, ideology has been important in the selection of the form of social policies.

LIBERALISM AND SOCIALISM AND THE DEVELOPMENT
OF WESTERN SOCIAL POLICY

As Western societies became industrialized, new systems of thought, including classical liberalism and socialism, were developed. Classical liberalism, as used in this context, does not have the same meaning that liberalism does in modern times. Classical liberalism, in the traditional sense, began as opposition to authoritarian rule. It focused on the needs of individuals and emphasized the values of individual freedom and equality. Early classical liberal thought stressed that individuals had an inherent right to seek private ends, including the possession of property. Classical liberals opposed strong central government.

Classical liberalism is associated with the introduction of the private market. Along with insisting that individuals should be free to participate in society, classical liberals felt that individuals should be responsible for themselves.[5] The individualist orientation is based on classical liberalism.

According to early socialist thought,[6] maintaining the social order takes precedence over establishing and supporting privately determined individual rights. Socialists feel that citizens should promote the general well-being. They believe that government should own some or all of the means of production and should be involved in comprehensive social and economic planning to benefit all of society.[7] Some aspects of socialist thought have contributed to the collectivist orientation.

These different philosophies, classical liberalism and socialism, have been important in the development of social welfare policy. Social welfare has been slower to develop in countries which are nonsocialist, such as the United States, which stressed the values of individual rights and responsibilities. In the United States, the individual was free earlier than in the socialist countries, such as Germany. However, there also has been less support for government social welfare measures to aid those who can not help themselves. Socialist societies, which stress the good of the group over that of the individual, naturally have been better able to develop social welfare policies sponsored by government than have societies which emphasize individual freedom and responsibility.[8]

This early conflict between the value of individual rights and responsibilities and the need for social policies administered by the government for the common good persists in modern times. It is a major constraint inhibiting the development of social welfare policy in the United States.

SOCIAL POLICY IN DIFFERENT POLITICAL AND ECONOMIC SYSTEMS

Societies differ in their political systems. In general, democracies, with their more cumbersome decision making procedures, can be slower to introduce social welfare measures than authoritarian societies. Interest groups tend to block one another in a democracy.[9] Further, when only a small percentage of the population will benefit from a specific social policy, it can be difficult to get a majority of the population to support a measure not in their immediate self-interest. For example, all taxpayers pay the cost of public welfare but only a small percentage of the population benefits directly from this social policy.

On the other hand, in a dictatorship, it can be easier to make the decision to institute social welfare measures. With the earliest and one of the broadest of the modern European social welfare systems, Germany provides a good example. Chancellor Bismark developed a social welfare system, in part to strengthen his power in the country.[10]

In dictatorships, social policies are controlled by the rulers and often used to strengthen their power in the country. For example, in the Soviet Union some social welfare benefits are available only to members of the Communist Party. In addition, those who oppose the rulers can be denied services such as medical care, pensions on retirements, and unemployment insurance. Political opponents can be diagnosed as mentally ill and jailed in mental institutions. Social policy is not used always for the best interest of clients. Social policy also can be employed to benefit authoritarian rulers.

Different types of social policies are found in industrialized societies with different economic structures. In a pure, free market economy, businesses are owned by private individuals. There is a belief that the production and distribution of goods and services are regulated best by the laws of supply and demand. In a market economy, social policy can serve the function of providing for the large numbers of people who are affected adversely by the workings of the free market.

On the other hand, there are economic arrangements where some or all of the means of production are owned by the government. Decisions about the production, distribution, and pricing of goods and services result from plans developed by public officials. For example, goals and objectives for the production of wheat and steel are developed by governmental officials. Farmers and factory workers are asked to produce enough to meet these goals. Theoretically, all workers are paid the same wage, and the products of their work are given to the state for sale and distribution to all of the people. Theoretically, under communism, there should be no social or economic differences among the workers, the managers, and the government leaders. Under communism, goods and services should be provided "to each, according to his need." Theoretically, one function of social welfare in a communist economy is to redistribute resources so that all are equal. In practice, while a classless society may be the ideal, there clearly are economic differences between the leaders and the led and the workers and the managers in communist societies.

Modern economies often are combinations of centralized planning and free market structures. Many communist societies are experimenting with providing economic incentives for productive workers and with allowing producers, such as farmers, to sell some of their produce on the open market for the best price they can get.

In both communist and free market economies, the government owns or has an active role in many economic enterprises. In the United States, for example, the government owns or influences the post office and part of the railroad industry. It regulates telephone companies, gas and electric companies, and television and radio stations. The government influences agricultural production and pricing. In the United States, the defense industry is totally dependent on government for its existence. It is now clear that there must be some intervention by government in the market economy.

Some Western socialist democracies, such as Sweden, seem to combine the best elements of the capitalist and socialist traditions. While the Swedish government owns some national industries, and helps others, there also is an active private sector. Although the work ethic in Sweden is very strong, there is also an extensive commitment to helping those in need.

For example, Sweden provides comprehensive medical and dental benefits, through the government, for all of its citizens. There are extensive retirement, disability, and unemployment policies. Pregnant women are allowed to stop working one month before giving birth and receive 90 percent of their salary. After the birth of a child, either the father or mother is allowed to take 6 months off from work to care for the child while receiving money called a parental benefit. The parental benefit is available also to parents who are unable to work because they have a child who is ten or under and needs special attention.[11] As a result, Sweden virtually has eliminated poverty and is ahead of the rest of the world in reducing many social problems. As Gunnar Heckscher writes, "As far as incomes are concerned, Sweden displays greater equality than any other Western country . . ."[12]

The benefits Swedes receive are paid for by high taxes. Sweden is the most taxed country in the world. The average Swede pays about half of his or her income to the government, while the average American pays about one-third of his or her income to government.[13]

Sweden's extensive social welfare benefits were developed during a period of economic expansion. As the Swedish economy has faltered, there have been some efforts to limit the growth of the welfare state.[14]

Sweden is much smaller than the United States in its population and geographic size. There is also greater homogeneity among its people. These factors ease the creation and functioning of social policy. Even with problems, Sweden's example proves that it is possible to provide extensive social welfare benefits, reduce inequality, and improve the general quality of life, while retaining freedom and democracy and private enterprise.

SOCIAL POLICY IN A CAPITALIST DEMOCRACY

There is a tension between the institutions of capitalism, democracy, and welfare in American society. This tension results from the different functions of these three institutions and from the different way in which they make decisions. The result is that in a democratic, capitalist society, there is support for social welfare policy, but there also are limits to the extent to which social policy can expand.

Capitalism creates the need for social welfare. This need exists because pure capitalism excludes from its benefits those who are unable to work. For those who do work, American capitalism has created significant social and economic inequalities.

Capitalism reaches its decisions through addition. Individual choices of consumers are added together by producers as they determine demand for their goods or services. Theoretically, there could be zero demand or almost infinite demand for a particular good or service.

Democracy is similar to capitalism in that citizens make individual choices about candidates who will represent their views on public policy questions. It is felt that if each individual citizen votes according to her or his own best interest, the good of the total society will be served.

Under democracy, a majority wins, and the minority agrees to accept the decision until the next election. In other words, over half of the participating voters must support a given candidate. The recipients of social policies are often numerical minorities, less than half of the electorate. For the needy to benefit in a democracy, voters must exhibit some degree of altruism.

Decisions in the marketplace are qualitatively different from decisions in the political sphere. The market gets its result by addition, by discovering the combined effects of expressed consumer wishes. The ballot reaches its conclusions by division, by having the minority accept the majority position.

Social welfare, however, is different from both the free market and democracy. It works to satisfy existing needs, often created by capitalism and found among a minority of the citizens. Decision making in welfare can be centralized and authoritarian.

In seeking to solve a social problem, social policy can describe rationally the social problem, the goals and objectives, and the best way to help those with a need. This analysis is undertaken most effectively and efficiently by a small group, hopefully with the best interests of clients as a guide. The solutions may be unpopular and, in most instances, will not benefit directly the majority of the citizens.[15]

In a democracy, then, social welfare asks voters to be altruistic. It asks voters to support the needs of the minority, whether this minority includes children, the unemployed, or the mentally and physically handicapped. Social policy asks voters to support efforts towards equality in the distribution of goods and services. This goal is the opposite of capitalism, because capitalism is based on the idea of private gain and produces inequality.[16]

In a capitalist democracy, there is some support for social welfare policies, because of both altruistic impulses and the fear of social disruption caused by inequality. But there also are limits to the degree to which social welfare can expand in a capitalist democracy. While extreme poverty can be eliminated, total equality never will be reached. There is support among voters to provide some help to those who cannot work and those who are very poor. However, there are limits to the extent to which citizens will vote for social policies which benefit others and which lessen the inequalities caused by capitalism.[17]

Pluralism and Social Policy

The need for centralized and sometimes authoritarian social planning creates tension in the relationship between social policy and democracy. Long-term, centralized social planning is in conflict with the major American values of participation and democracy. In a democratic and pluralistic society, social policy decisions may be responsive to prevailing values and may benefit strong interest groups and agencies. But social policy decisions reached through a pluralistic approach, which can accommodate the most powerful parties, agencies, and individuals, do not necessarily make for the most effective and efficient social welfare policies. Through the pluralistic approach of accommodating the most powerful interest groups, social policies often are developed which benefit these interest groups rather than clients. As Allen Schick writes, pluralistic decision making tends to reinforce the status quo.[18]

An analogy can be drawn with the area of physical planning. In many communities, there has been little physical planning. Houses, stores, and businesses are located next to each other. Everyone pursues his or her own individual interests, with little concern for the overall good of the community.

In contrast, there are communities where residential areas are separated from stores and businesses. Zoning authorities have the right to determine land use. Here, decision making is centralized to provide for a better overall community. This centralization restricts, to some extent, the freedom of the individual, who might want to expand a business or put a business in a home. But this restriction on individual rights is agreed to in order to protect the overall good of the community.

Social policy development faces the same dilemma as physical planning. The dilemma is that centralized planning permits the best possible social policy but, in the process, restricts individual freedoms and the pursuit of individual interests.

SUMMARY

Social policy is a concomitant of industrialization and is found in all modern societies. Social policies are either universal or selective. Social policies exist in democracies and dictatorships and in capitalist and socialist economies. The scope and function of social policy vary according to the economic, political, and social organization of the society.

Social policy is needed in a capitalist democracy because the free market does not provide for those unable to work, and the free market creates large social and economic inequalities. If voters are altruistic, there can be some support for social policy in a democracy. Social policy asks citizens to vote for help for minorities; for those who comprise less than half of the voting population.

Decision making in social welfare tends to be centralized

and should be based on client needs. Decision making in a democracy tends to be decentralized and influenced heavily by interest groups. These groups can be destructive to the development of efficient and effective social policies based on client need.

Generally, democratic, individually oriented societies oppose centralized, long-range planning which can be characteristic of effective social policy. This structural dilemma results in some waste, inefficiency, and ineffectiveness in social welfare programs. This dilemma is a major problem facing social policy development in a democracy.

NOTES

1. Gaston Rimlinger, *Welfare Policy and Industrialization in Europe, America and Russia.* New York: John Wiley & Sons, 1971.

2. *Ibid.*

3. *Ibid.*

4. Robert M. Moroney, Policy Analysis Within a Value Theoretical Framework, In Ron Haskins & James J. Gallagher, (eds.), *Models for Analysis Of Social Policy: An Introduction.* Norwood, N.J.: ABLEX Publishing Co., 1981, pp. 94–97.

5. Dorothy James, Materialistic Individualism and Ethnocentrism. In *Poverty, Politics, and Change,* New Jersey: Prentice-Hall, Inc. 1972, pp. 22–39.

6. *Ibid.*

7. *Ibid.*

8. Rimlinger, *ibid.*

9. *Ibid.*

10. *Ibid.*

11. Alan J. Gilderson & Eva Marshall, *Social Benefits in Sweden.* Stockholm, Sweden: The Swedish Institute, 1973.

12. Gunnar Heckscher, What is the Purpose of Welfare? *Social Change In Sweden,* May 1972, *25,* p. 4.

13. Pia Brandelius, *Election Year '79: Taxes—One of the Main Issues in the 1979 Election.* Stockholm, Sweden: The Swedish Institute, 1979.

14. Ruth Arne, *The End of the Swedish Model?* Stockholm, Sweden: The Swedish Institute, 1980.

15. T.H. Marshall, Value Problems of Welfare-Capitalism. *Journal of Social Policy,* January 1972, pp. 15–32.

16. Richard Titmuss, *The Gift of Blood Relationship; From Human Blood to Social Policy.* New York: Pantheon Books, 1971.

17. Marshall, *ibid.*

18. Allen Schick, Systems Politics and Systems Budgeting. *Public Administration Review,* March/April 1969, pp. 137–151.

Part III

THE DEVELOPMENT OF
MODERN SOCIAL POLICY

Chapter 6

COOPERATION AND CHARITY—THE BEGINNINGS OF SOCIAL WELFARE

INTRODUCTION

The social policies of today can be seen as having their base partly in the early social experiences of tribes and of families. As society became more complex, aid to those in need was formalized as a part of religious and philosophical viewpoints. The breakup of feudalism and the rise of the market economy created major social, economic, and political dislocations. Building on earlier traditions, social welfare emerged in the market economy as an institution necessary to the functioning of society.[1]

The development of social welfare policy has not been always orderly. Each new policy has not been always an improvement over its predecessor. In fact, many social policies have been more concerned with social control than with helping those in need. Further, while broad events, such as the breakup of feudalism, were very significant in the development of social policy, local, regional, and national factors were important in creating variations in social policy in Western society.[2]

Early Social Welfare Efforts

The earliest form of social organization was the tribe—the first small group. To survive in a hostile environment, prehistoric individuals had to work together and cooperate. Without cooperation and mutual support efforts, the tribe would perish. These early examples of cooperation and mutual support became ingrained in human social organization. The impulses to work with others for the survival of the group and to help out others in time of need were the earliest manifestations of social welfare.

The family, especially the early extended family, provided help to those who needed it. Families took care of the aged and the sick, and relatives raised children whose parents had died. Because everyone worked, there was no unemployment.[3] Our modern social welfare system can be traced to early cooperation and mutual support efforts found in the tribe and the family.

As groups grew larger and society became more complex, some of these early efforts at cooperation and mutual support were institutionalized through organized religion. Early religious teachings contributed a humanitarian ethic regarding the care of those in need. Religion took on social welfare functions and probably gave social welfare some of its altruistic values.[4]

The Jewish people had an early concern for those in need. Early Jewish tribes from the time of Abraham, around the seventeenth century B.C., had developed informal mutual support efforts. The first formal Jewish social welfare arrangements occurred during the time of David, around 1,000 B.C. It was felt that God ordered help to the needy.[5] The prophet Isaiah told the Jewish people, "share your bread with the hungry and bring the homeless poor into your house." Throughout the Old Testament, which dates back to the tenth century B.C., there were commandments to be charitable to the sick, the old, the handicapped, and the poor. All who could afford to were obliged to give charity. Similarly, those who were in need were obliged to take charity. The Talmud, a collection of Jewish law and tradition, compiled around 500 A.D. and still important to many Jews, states that a poor person should be given enough charity to satisfy his needs. The Talmud also describes how charitable monies are to be raised and distributed and specifies the need for a tax collector to administer the system. The famous Jewish scholar and philosopher, Maimonides (1204–1135 B.C.) wrote that individuals who had too much pride to accept charity were responsible for their own suffering and were guilty of bloodshed, sin, or both.

Jews have had a historic concern for children. They made the care of dependent children a special duty under law. Jews placed orphans in selected family homes. This early practice of child placement was taken up by the Christian Church.[6] For example, the early Christian Church would board children with "worthy widows" and pay for their care through collections. Child placement was a substantial program, because the persecutions by Roman emperors resulted in many homeless children.[7]

As early as 400 B.C., Buddhism emphasized love and charity. The Koran, the seventh century A.D. sacred text of Islam, promotes cooperative and mutual support efforts. The Koran stresses that charity should be shown to travelers, widows, orphans, and the needy. According to the Koran, the giving of alms, or money to the poor, is one of the five most important obligations of Islam. Those who practice almsgiving will go to heaven.[8]

Christianity built on early Hebrew and Greek thought. Christianity emphasized that distress should be relieved and that charity was important for the individual in need, the giver, and the community. Jesus told his Disciples, "give to everyone who begs from you." The teachings of St. Paul, St. Augustine, St. Bernard, St. Francis, and St. Thomas Aquinas gave poverty a kind of dignity and supported the granting of alms to the needy. The poor were accepted because suffering and poverty were redemptive. Those in need were seen as desirable recipients of this religious act.[9]

Secular authorities also participated in developing social policies. As early as 1,700 B.C. in Babylonia, Hammurabi's Code (which was based on the laws of Ur-nammu, Lipit-Ishtar and Bilalama some 100 to 200 years earlier) made provisions for hospitality for strangers and the protection of widows, orphans, and the weak. The early Greeks and Romans provided daily payments for the crippled, institutions for orphans and others, and the public distribution of grain for the needy. In fact, the words charity and philanthropy, and the ideas upon which they are based, humanity, brotherhood, and love for mankind, are of Greek origin.

The early philosophers supported and promoted humanitarian ideas. Aristotle (384–322 B.C.) felt that man was a social being who, by his nature, had to cooperate with others. Aristotle felt that it was more noble to give than to receive. Cicero (143–106 B.C.) thought that a just society required that people be merciful towards each other. Everyone should be consulted and have an opportunity to participate in society.[10]

After the fall of the Roman Empire, the administration of help for the poor was concentrated in the Church. Help came from monasteries and hospitals administered by the Church. Support for the needy in their own homes was found at the parish level. Begging flourished because the giving of alms was supported by religious doctrine.

Many religious leaders, including St. Francis, endorsed begging. Begging was practiced by friars, pilgrims to or from the Holy Land, and even university scholars. It is significant that the giving of alms was a religious act done not so much to help the poor as to obey God's commandment. The focus was on the giver of the gift and his or her salvation, rather than on the recipient of the gift.

Beginning in the sixth century, monasteries became important agencies for relief, especially in rural areas. Some monasteries had as their major purpose helping the needy. Monasteries gave to anyone who appeared at their doors, and in some cases, provided food and other provisions in the community. Some monasteries educated children, housed women and children, and provided lodging to travelers. However, there was little coordination between the monasteries. Their charity was unorganized and indiscriminate. By the middle 1300s, there were hundreds of monasteries in England which provided some social services. These monasteries varied in size from 12 to 200 inhabitants.

Early hospitals often were attached to monasteries. Hospitals usually were supported by gifts from the wealthy. In addition to providing medical assistance, hospitals housed the elderly, orphans, and the poor and often cared for travelers. However, hospitals often were administered badly and sometimes were breeding grounds for disease.

Extensive poor relief was administered by church officials at the diocese or parish level. The bishop of each diocese was responsible for feeding and protecting the district's poor. Usually, the parish priest provided this care. When possible, recipients lived in the community, outside of an institution. This form of help was termed outdoor relief.

Tithing provided most of the funds for the charitable efforts of the church. In England, one-third of the funds which the church received were designated for the poor. The tithe was codified in the law of King Ethelred in 1014.[11]

Feudalism was the basic social, economic, and political system of the Middle Ages. Feudalism started in Europe around 800 A.D. and vestiges of it remained in Europe until 1500. Under feudalism, a lord had a castle, the surrounding manor, and serfs to work the land. The manor was a self-supporting economic unit. Technically, the lord's power came from the king. However, because the king was weak, especially during early feudalism, each lord actually had almost complete power over his lands and the people who worked them.

The life of the serf was hard and unchanging. The crops and animals tended by the serf belonged to the lord, and only a portion of both were for consumption by serfs. It was difficult to change one's position in life—once a serf, always a serf. There was little thought of competition or of private gain.

The lords ultimately were responsible for their serfs. The serfs were seen as valuable property and were provided with minimal care so that they could work. The serfs were assured the bare necessities of life. Serfs had the right to live on the land and to work it, but they could not leave it. Lords were responsible for providing for the elderly. If a serf died, his wife and children had certain rights. During open-house several times a year, the lords would feed and entertain all comers. In addition, lords provided hospitality to travelers and gave alms to the poor. Both acts were part of their religious duty.

The relationship between the feudal lord and his serf was essentially paternalistic and included some aspects of the unilateral transfer. The lord provided land and shelter. The lord had all of the power and wealth and made grants and gifts to the peasants. In contrast to today's working conditions, it was difficult for a serf to better himself substantially or look elsewhere for work. On the other hand, the feudal lord was ultimately responsible for taking care of and protecting all of the serfs. There was a degree of security in the serf's life. The serf almost always had a job if he wanted it, and he generally could depend on the lord for physical safety. This security was to change with the breakup of feudalism and the growth of a market economy.

City life was different from life on the manor. In the city, freemen, merchants, and craftsmen were beginning to establish a market economy. As independent entrepreneurs, craftsmen determined wages and prices. They also regulated entry into their trades and came together to form associations or guilds which emphasized self-help and cooperation. Among other functions, the guilds provided social welfare benefits, including a kind of social insurance program which supported members who were unable to work. In addition, pensions were provided for the families of deceased members. While these benefits were primarily for guild members, some guilds sponsored works of charity for the poor.[12]

During the early development of social welfare services, help offered was limited, often inadequate, and available only for the most needy. For most, life was extremely hard, and only the barest necessities were available. Still, there was some support for early efforts to help those who could not help themselves. These initial attempts at social service were the beginnings of our present social policies.

THE BREAKUP OF FEUDALISM AND THE RISE OF A MARKET ECONOMY

The growth of secular control started in the thirteenth century. The disorganization and corruption of the church was one catalyst. Another was the desire of secular authorities to control charitable endowments. Secular control resulted in the dissolution of the monasteries, one of the major sources of help for the poor during feudalism. Hospitals were taken over by municipalities.

As feudalism was weakened, serfs migrated to the growing cities. The increasing opportunity for travel provided more freedom for the individual. Since England was heavily forested and not densely populated, it was relatively easy for an individual to escape from a manor to freedom. During harvests, there were great hordes of migratory laborers. The opportunity to travel and the availability of work tended to weaken further the feudal relationship between a lord and his serf. Wars with France provided the individual with an opportunity to leave his home and relocate in a new community.

As Europe emerged from feudalism, new issues confronted society. Questions arose, such as, did a man own himself?, could a man sell property?, could a man marry off his children without his lord's consent?, and, could a man leave the community in which he was born, and if he did, could his lord bring him back?[13]

Under feudalism, the life of the worker was relatively stable. Except for war and famine, the economy generally was undisturbed. For the serf, life was both relatively secure and unchanging. However, "with the breaking of the old system came the separation of men from the land and the beginning of movement. Thereby men escaped their bondage at the price of their security."[14]

The development of towns and of factories and the increase in commerce brought new relationships which were more susceptible to serious disturbance. The old, self-contained feudal manor was replaced by more complex and interdependent relationships. The period was one of dislocation—dislocation of worker from land, home, and lifelong jobs. For the first time, workers were subjected to seasonal employment, underemployment, and casual employment. According to Carl de Schweinitz, ". . . an industrial civilization would be baffled by the problem of how to provide him (the worker) with an equivalent of the provision against sickness, old age, and the other personal exigencies which, however inadequate, had been the corollary of his serf-dom. These were the circumstances under which . . . pover-ty became a concern of government."[15] As W.K. Jordan writes, "So convulsive was this long period that a once stable society was torn apart and masses of men—the dispossessed, the mas-terless, and the incompetent—were literally set in motion by ir-resistible forces as they sought first work that was not to be had and then alms which society was neither equipped nor disposed to give."[16]

The replacement of feudalism with capitalism was one of the most basic and widespread changes in Western history. For the first time, an individual was not guaranteed a job. Workers with skills which were in demand by the society could sell their labor and make money. Individuals whose skills were not in de-mand had almost nowhere to turn for the necessities of life. There was no feudal lord to provide food, shelter, work, and physical protection. Unemployed individuals could beg, steal, or starve. Under the market economy, the laws of the marketplace, of supply and demand, ruled.

Since the breakup of feudalism, Western society has strug-gled with the consequences of the market economy. For some of those able and willing to work, capitalism has provided a chance for personal advancement, relative wealth, and a degree of power and freedom unknown under feudalism. For those un-able to work because they were handicapped or because society did not value their labor, capitalism created social problems which have yet to be resolved.

As capitalism developed in England and in other Europe-an countries, it became clear that the market economy could not provide for those who could not or did not work. The his-tory of the poor laws is the history of many, often contradictory efforts, to determine what was appropriate for those who were not able to work or to receive a living wage. A generally accept-able solution is not yet in sight. However, over time, there has been a growing consensus that in a market economy, some help should be given to those who cannot provide for them-selves because of their inability to work or because of the lack of jobs.

Summary

Modern social policies can trace their beginnings to the need for mutual support and cooperation inherent in prehistoric human social organization. Early philosophy and religion supported efforts by society for those in need. With the rise of feudalism, serfs gained the security of life on the manor along with the inability to change a poor and oppressed style of living. Help for the needy was provided primarily by the church through charity.

With the breakup of feudalism, serfs gained a degree of freedom and individual responsibility. However, people had to contend with the uncertainties of surviving in a market economy which seemed inherently unstable. While it is clear that since recorded history there were social welfare efforts to help those in need, they were generally inadequate and disorganized. Life for the vast majority of people was extremely difficult.

Notes

1. The author would like to acknowledge the help of Dr. James Cronin, Department of History, University of Wisconsin Milwaukee, who made many helpful comments on this and the subsequent chapter, and of Richard C. Lux, Assistant Professor of Scripture, Sacred Heart School of Theology, Hales Corners, Wisconsin, who made many helpful comments on the religious section of this chapter.

2. David A. Rochefort, Progressive and Social Control Perspectives on Social Welfare, *Social Service Review,* December, 1981, pp. 568–592.

3. Charles S. Prigmore, & Charles R. Atherton. *Social Welfare Policy: Analysis and Formulation.* Lexington, Mass.: D.C. Heath & Co., 1979.

4. Prigmore, Atherton, *ibid.*

5. Walter Trattner, *From Poor Law to Welfare State: A History of Social Welfare in America.* New York: The Free Press, 1979.

6. Prigmore, Atherton, *ibid.*

7. Trattner, *ibid.*

8. Karl de Schweinitz, *England's Road to Social Security.* New York: A.S. Barnes & Co., Inc., 1961, p. 17.

9. Trattner, *ibid.*

10. de Schweinitz, *ibid.,* p. 17.

11. Prigmore, Atherton, *ibid.*

12. *Ibid.*

13. de Schweinitz, *ibid.,* p. 12.

14. *Ibid.,* p. 13.

15. W.K. Jordan, *Philanthropy in England 1480–1660: A Study of the Changing Pattern of English Social Aspirations.* New York: Russell Sage Foundation, 1959, pp. 55–56.

16. *Ibid.*

Chapter 7

EARLY SOCIAL POLICY—THE ENGLISH POOR LAW

INTRODUCTION

The social policies of today are direct descendants of English Poor Law and its predecessors. Some very basic social welfare distinctions, such as the difference between the deserving and undeserving poor, were developed during and after the breakup of feudalism. These early approaches exert a powerful influence on modern social policy. Today's hospitals, prisons, sheltered workshops, community care arrangements, public assistance programs, and programs for children and for the elderly are based on similar programs developed during this period. Welfare reform experiments dating back to the postfeudal period are being studied today as policy makers search for better approaches in public welfare. Some knowledge of this past is necessary to understand the social policies of today.

THE ORDINANCE OF LABOURERS OF 1349

In the early 1300s, a devastating famine swept through England. By 1349, the bubonic plague had killed more than one-third of the total population. The famine and the plague resulted in a serious reduction in the supply of labor. Workers were able to demand high wages, observe holidays, and bargain for higher wages from competing employers. Workers who survived the famine and the bubonic plague enjoyed a freedom and power which they had not known before.

Agriculture was seriously affected. The rich landowners longed to return to the old feudal ways when serfs were tied to the land and to the landowner.

The breakup of feudalism and the growth of the power of the working class led to the Ordinance of Labourers of 1349. Often regarded as the first Poor Law, the Ordinance of Labourers was an attempt to regulate begging and the movement of workers. It was aimed at controlling both begging and what the landowners felt were the undesirable consequences of the shortage of workers.

The Ordinance of Labourers provided that no worker could be paid more than a specified maximum wage and forbade the worker to travel from community to community. These proscriptions eliminated competiton among employers. In an effort to decrease begging and force beggars into the work force, the Ordinance of Labourers prevented the private donor from giving charity to whomever he chose.

Further regulations in 1377 and 1388 dealt with relief to the non-able-bodied poor. These regulations reflected a new recognition that the non-able-bodied poor, such as the old or the handicapped, had a right to relief. They became the responsibility of the local communities. The non-able-bodied poor were given the right to travel from community to community if they had official approval. They were allowed to beg. The earlier restriction on travel of the able-bodied poor was reaffirmed in these regulations.

The Ordinance of Labourers of 1349, and the subsequent regulations probably were too stringent to be enforced strictly. However, they contributed to establishing the basis of the English and eventually the American social welfare systems. Many of the components of our current social welfare system can be traced to these early statutes.

The Ordinance of Labourers and the subsequent related regulations made a basic distinction between the undeserving able-bodied and the deserving non-able-bodied poor. Today, as during the time of the Poor Law, society is more generous in the help that it provides to the non-able-bodied deserving poor and more punitive to the so-called able-bodied poor. For example, under the Social·Security system, support for the aged poor, the blind, and the disabled is seen as a right. A monthly check provided by the federal government is guaranteed to all recipients of the program, regardless of where they live.

On the other hand, society continues to be punitive towards those who appear to be able to work. These are called the undeserving poor. They include men, women, and teenagers who receive help under locally financed general assistance programs or under the Aid to Families with Dependent Children Program (AFDC). Grants are low, and there usually is a stigma attached to the receipt of help. There is no federally prescribed minimum grant level. Consequently, the level of the grant varies from state to state. All states pay less than is adequate, though some grants are more inadequate than others. Extremely low payments are found especially in the South and Southwest.

The Ordinance of Labourers of 1349 and the additional regulations of 1377 and 1388 are also an early example of the close relationship between social policy and labor market policy. In an effort to increase the supply of able-bodied laborers, the Ordinance of Labourers attempted to accomplish an economic purpose through a social policy. By denying aid to the able-bodied, it attempted to force them to work. The social policy specified who could and who could not receive charity from the community.

PUNITIVE APPROACHES TO SOCIAL CONTROL

In the early 1500s, the supply of unskilled labor increased dramatically. This increase resulted from several factors. With the growth of stronger central governments, there were fewer wars between nobles, and therefore, more able-bodied men available for work. No famines and plagues comparable to those of the 1300s, reduced the population. The growth of textile manufacturing brought the enclosure movement. The enclosure movement, which began in the late 1500s, literally enclosed the fields with fences. People were forced out of their houses to make way for grazing sheep. The population moving into towns swelled the urban supply labor.

Textile manufacturing, which replaced the earlier crafts, was characterized by frequent expansions and contractions. Frequent expansion and contraction were true of agriculture also. A large number of workers were needed, especially in the spring and in the fall, but they were unemployed during the winter. Society had to cope with the fact of seasonal, intermittent employment in agriculture and in textiles and the consequent problem of caring for unemployed workers.

Later in the 1500s, the importation of silver from the New World resulted in substantial inflation. Inflation had the most serious effect on the poor and unskilled seasonal workers, since they could not buy as much with their money.

Two results of the population shift to the towns, intermittant employment, and inflation, were a significant increase in unskilled labor and a noticeable increase in begging. Laws to repress begging became more stringent and punitive. In the 1300s the purpose of the laws was to force beggars into the work force. By the 1500s the main purpose of social policy was social control. The work force was already too large by the sixteenth century.

In London, for example, between 1514 and 1524, there were a series of regulations concerning beggars, vagrants, and vagabonds. Beggars and vagrants were licensed by town officials, and vagabonds had the letter "V" fastened to their chest. Vagabonds were driven through the town with a horn sounding before them. Eventually, they were chained as they went through the city. They were allowed to receive alms; unlicensed beggars were not.[1] The licensing of beggars in order to control them still persists in some of the larger cities in the United States.

It was felt that the physically fit should work and that harsh measures should be taken against those who were idle. For example, a 1552 law stated, "if any man or woman, able to work, should refuse to labour and live idly for three days, he or she should be branded with a red hot iron on the breast with the letter "V" and should be judged the slave for two years of any person who should inform against such idler."[2] In 1572 a law was passed which gave a broad definition of begging and prescribed serious punishments. On first offense, punishment could include "burning through the gristle of the right ear."[3] A third offense could be punished by death.

However, while it continued the earlier distinction between the deserving and the undeserving poor, the 1572 law, for the first time, provided also the statutory authority for local officials to tax residents to pay for poor relief. Local judges taxed town residents, and the judges were given the power to place in jail individuals who did not pay their poor relief taxes.

THE POOR LAW OF 1601

During the sixteenth century, the church, in the past the major institution to help those in need, was poorer and less effective in providing charity. The monasteries were dissolved in the middle 1500s. The state began to intervene and made paying for the care of the poor a compulsory responsibility for landowners. The increase of public administration of poor relief came during this period. Many religious hospitals were taken over by towns and operated by local, public administrators, known as Governors of the Poor.

The efforts to punish begging through the use of force did not work. If someone was hungry and there was no job available, the individual had few alternatives. Gradually, legislators gave up the idea that the poor were to blame totally for their own poverty and that they could be forced out of it.

During the late 1500s there was a serious shortage of grain. Some farmers kept their grain from the market in order to raise the price. Low income people had a particularly hard time affording food, and there were rebellions in many towns across

England. To deal with this problem, Parliament first tried to force farmers, in 1572 and again in 1587, to bring their grain to market. In addition, Parliament tried to get farmers to sell their grain at a reasonable price. When these efforts were ineffectual, an attempt was made to organize the supply of grain so that it could be sold throughout the year. These policies showed recognition, for the first time, that the poor were not to blame totally for their condition. Economic and social factors contributed to poverty.

With inflation and low wages, beginning efforts were made to supplement the income of workers by providing them with money or supplies, in addition to their earnings. For example, in 1575, arrangements were made to supplement wages by providing wool, flax, and hemp to every town to give to the able-bodied.

The introduction of the idea of supplements to the wages of the working poor was a major and significant event. The idea of supplementing persisted and was developed extensively in the 1700s under plans such as the one developed in Speenhamland in 1795. What to do with the low-paid, able-bodied poor has been a persistent problem in social policy. It remains unresolved.

In 1597, Parliament passed several bills dealing with management of the poor. The bills were to form the basis of what later became known as the English Poor Laws. Together, these bills organized management of aid to the poor. The laws placed the relief of the non-able-bodied, deserving poor in the hands of church wardens and four public officials who were called Overseers of the Poor. The laws made the Overseers of the Poor responsible for providing work for able-bodied, unemployed adults and for parentless children who could be apprenticed. The laws provided for the operation of old age homes, called hospitals, for the elderly. The laws established workhouses for "sturdy beggars, rogues, and vagabonds." If they were not sent to these institutions, beggars could be indentured to a businessman or banished from the community. If the beggars returned, they would be killed. Finally, the laws provided legal authority for the taxing of all property owners to pay for these policies.

These laws were consolidated in 1601 into a law which commonly is thought of as defining the major aspects of English Poor Law. The 1601 Law was the result of several hundred years of discussion and evolution. In addition to incorporating the provisions of previous laws, the 1601 law established governmental responsibility for poor relief at the central government level, the county magistrate level, and the local parish level.[4]

Essentially, the English Poor law divided the poor into three major categories. The poor by incapacity and defect included the aged, the disabled, the blind, and the mentally ill. They deserved community help. Where possible, this help was outdoor relief, provided in the community. Recipients lived in their own homes or those of friends or neighbors and were provided with enough to sustain them.

The second group was the poor by casualty. The poor by casualty included those who had lost their property because of some catastrophe. This group included disabled persons who could work and some children. Along with some of the poor by incapacity and defect, they lived in workhouses and worked at jobs contracted with private business.

Finally, there were the thriftless poor. These were alcoholics, rioters, and unacceptable beggars. They were sent to jails, known as houses of correction.[5]

In many respects, the Poor Law of 1601, like earlier laws, was harsh and punitive. One of its main purposes was social control. As Geoffrey Oxley writes, ". . . the problem of poverty became an integral part of the problem of law and order, the maintenance of which was essential to the continuance of effective government. . . . The central aim of this policy was the suppression of vagrancy and the begging that went with it."[6]

In 1662, the British Parliament passed the Act of Settlement and Removal, which Norman Longmate feels was ". . . possibly the worst law ever passed by a British Parliament."[7] The Act of 1662, and subsequent revisions in 1686 and 1692, tried to regulate travel, so that the poor could not move from town to town to get charity. The provisions were complicated and difficult to administer. These laws did establish the principle that while the poor were not allowed to travel to get charity without the permission of the authorities, the town of their origin had responsibility to take care of them.[8]

THE WORKHOUSE

The workhouse was an institution whose residents did some work on the premises. It housed some of the low-skilled poor. Workhouses received legal sanction as early as 1597. They often were administered privately because of the great expense to a parish to build a workhouse. In the 1600s, increasing destitution among the population led to the building of workhouses in most communities.

Almost any place where the poor were housed was designated as a workhouse. Sometimes they were called poorhouses or almshouses. The typical workhouse had between 20 and 50 residents. These included the non-able-bodied poor, children who were not placed in foster care, the handicapped, the retarded, the mentally ill, pregnant women without supportive family, and the elderly. Workhouses housed and fed all those who could not survive on outdoor relief.

The smaller workhouses were administered by a pauper inmate. In medium-sized communities, one job of a professional parish officer was administration of the workhouses. The largest workhouses were administered by a professional manager. In some parishes, the management of the workhouse was contracted out to a private operator. Successful administration of the workhouse involved minimizing both expenses and the complaints of the inmates to the authorities.

The workhouses were the predecessors of our current sheltered workshops. Certain private businesses, usually related in England to the manufacture of cloth, would pay the workhouse for jobs undertaken by the inmates. Some of the inmates worked for the workhouse manager. Most of the teachers and social welfare workers of the time were paupers employed by the workhouse manager. The workhouses generally were not self-sufficient and had to be subsidized by the parish.

Conditions in the workhouses varied widely. They often were unsanitary. In some houses, life was harsh. In others, contrary to popular opinion, life was generally pleasant and congenial, similar to living in an extended family. Generally, parishes attempted to keep their able-bodied poor on outdoor relief, because workhouses were expensive to operate. The workhouse was reserved for those who needed institutional care.[9]

Similar to the workhouses were houses of correction, or jails, to correct those who, it was felt, needed discipline. In 1609 to 1910 a law provided that one or more houses of correction were to be erected in every county for "rogues and other idle persons." Perhaps the most famous was Bridewell, in London. Inmates worked in textiles and other crafts. Any two of the governors of Bridewell had the power to take into it any person whom they thought was idle or lewd. The Governors had the power to search all places where "masterless" men might congregate, and they could punish landlords or tenants who harbored them.

SPEENHAMLAND—AN EARLY GUARANTEED ANNUAL INCOME

Toward the end of the 1700s, England was experiencing serious poverty in the face of rapid industrialization. While a few people were accumulating unprecedented wealth, the vast majority of the population were poor. Poverty was more serious among rural workers than among urban workers, who could take advantage of manufacturing opportunities to improve their conditions.

Pressure to assist the rural poor came from two sources. Without their farm labor, a rural community would not have sufficient food. Further, supplementing the income of the rural poor discouraged them from socially disruptive begging or stealing.

In order to help the poor, villages paid supplements. These supplements started in the 1500s and became more widespread in the 1700s. They are the predecessor of our modern income transfer programs, such as AFDC and General Assistance.

At one time or another, during the last part of the eighteenth century, almost every parish in southern England had adopted some form of subsidy. For example, in 1771, the village of Parkhurst supplemented wages up to 25 percent of earnings. In 1783, the justices of the parish of Whittlesford decided that every man who had a family and "behaves himself seemly" be given money to buy bread for himself and his family.[10]

These subsidies could take many different forms. In some communities, when the price of flour was high, it was sold to the poor at reduced rates. In other communities, commodities were given to the poor. Finally, some communities supplemented the wages of able-bodied workers.[11]

Perhaps the most famous of these efforts occured in Speenhamland. On May 6, 1795, the Justices of Berkshire met at an inn in Speenhamland. The original intention of the Justices was to establish wage rates for day laborers. Many argued for raising the wage rates. However, the Justices finally agreed to an elaborate system of wage supplementation. Every man was given an amount of money to supplement his wages. The amount was tied in part to the price of bread. The supplement rose and fell in direct relation to the rise and fall of bread prices. What became known as the Speenhamland Scales was tied to the rate of inflation. Also, the amount of money which supplemented the low wages was tied to the size of a man's family. More money was provided to those with bigger families.[12]

Speenhamland has come to be identified with all of the efforts toward the end of the eighteenth century in England to supplement low wages. It is important today, because it is the model upon which modern income maintenance proposals, such as the Guaranteed Annual Income and the Negative Income Tax, are based. While debated since the 1960s, these policies never have been implemented in the United States.

Even conservative economists, such as Milton Friedman, have proposed a negative income tax for the poor. This support of some government intervention in the private marketplace is based on early experiments such as Speenhamland. In the market economy which was developing in the eighteenth century, policy makers saw and acted on the need for some outside support from the community to help those who could not survive. This development is extremely important, because it is a major rationale for the existence of social welfare in a capitalist economy.

The consequences of Speenhamland still are debated today. Critics charge that wage supplementation supported employers who did not pay adequate wages. These critics assert that the provision of money or bread paid for by community-raised taxes eliminated any incentive for some employers to pay a higher wage. The same criticisms are made today of programs which force welfare recipients, as a condition of their grant, to accept jobs in the private sector at less than the minimum wage.

Other critics charged that employees worked less hard when they knew that their low wages would be supplemented by the community. However, the increase agricultural yields and a strong demand for labor during this period refute the argument.[13]

Some historians believe that "outdoor relief appears, on balance, to have functioned as an income subsidy rather than a wage subsidy; that is to say, the amount of relief given depended on need rather than the quantity of labor supplied."[14] The subsidies were individualized. They took into account family size, the health of the family, and its general economic condition.

Generally, poor relief brought people up to near subsistence levels during the early 1800s. Some communities paid regular amounts to those in need, while in others, the supplements were more sporadic.

THE POOR LAW REFORM ACT OF 1834

The end of the war with France resulted in a surplus of labor. A nationwide investigation into the Poor Law was established. The Poor Law Inquiry Commissioners, who were highly ideological, blamed the increase in workers incorrectly on the effects of Speenhamland and similar programs. Although they did not conduct a thorough and factual investigation into the Poor Law, the Poor Law Inquiry Commissioners concluded that the supplement programs, such as Speenhamland, were expensive and had negative effects on workers. The Commissioners recommended the termination of outdoor relief.[15]

As a result the Poor Law Reform Act of 1834, was enacted. It abolished all aid for the able-bodied poor. This was a harsh act inspired more by ideological considerations than by an objective investigation of the facts.

The Poor Law Reform Act of 1834 was one of the most punitive of the English Poor Laws. It restricted home relief and administered the workhouse under the most severe conditions possible.

The English Poor Law Reform Act of 1834 was based in part on the thought of the Reverend Thomas Malthus, the founder of modern population theory. Malthus believed that the population increased geometrically, while the food supply increased only arithmetically. To solve this problem he felt that the poor should be considered expendable. Malthus argued that social welfare programs should be terminated so that the poor would not continue to propagate. He believed that overpopulation caused poverty. In short, the poor were responsible for their own condition.[16] Since it was unrealistic, the Poor Law Reform Act of 1834 generally was ignored. Many who had received outdoor relief were placed in workhouses. In rural areas, supplements were continued, ostensibly in aid of sickness rather than to supplement wages.

Under the Poor Law Reform Act of 1834, parishes were retained as the administrative unit for poor relief. Help was provided for the deserving poor. In addition, during slack economic times, parishes hired workers to supplement their income. As Anne Digby writes, "The use of poor-law allowances to relieve the able-bodied poor in their own homes continued to be used after 1834 as one form of accommodating the problem of surplus labor."[17]

The Poor Law Reform Act of 1834 did limit the growth of the public sector in social policy. This limit stimulated the growth of private charities. Some of these charities aided the members of a particular occupation. Other charities provided bread, coal, money, and medical attention to the poor and others in need. A particularly generous example is provided by the experience in Nottingham, England, where there were 51 "friendly societies." These societies provided various kinds of help to members, including medical services, care and education for orphans, and care for the elderly. The Charities in Nottingham were quite extensive. They owned 622 acres of land, 163 houses, and invested almost 40,000 pounds. This investment yielded over 2,000 pounds in income a year. Of this amount, over half was given directly to the poor. The rest was used to support almshouses and 15 hospitals which accommodated 160 elderly people. Another charity in Nottingham supported, through bequests and some user fees, approximately 1,000 patients a year.[18]

The growth of the private sector eventually resulted in the establishment of the Charity Organization Societies, the predecessors of our modern Family Service Agencies, and of the Settlement Houses.

Summary

Many of our modern social policies are based on the English Poor Laws. As early as 1349, the Ordinance of Labourers identified the non-able-bodied poor as deserving of community help. For those who were able-bodied, the Ordinance of Labourers prohibited begging. In order to keep wages down during a period of labor scarcity, the Ordinance of Labourers established maximum wages and prohibited workers from traveling freely from community to community in search of high-paying jobs.

As the supply of labor outstripped the demand for labor, more punitive measures were instituted to insure social stability. The care of the poor was taken over from religious officials and became an important function of government. The Poor Law of 1601 incorporated earlier laws which established public officials, called Overseers of the Poor, who were responsible for a community's social welfare system. Outdoor relief for those who could live in the community, workhouses for those who needed institutional care, and jails, or houses of correction, for those who were dangerous, were all part of the social welfare system of the time.

At the beginning of the eighteenth century, poverty increased. This increase was responded to by more extensive outdoor relief, which was available to the deserving unemployed and to the low-paid working poor. Sometimes, as in Speenhamland, the supplements were pegged to the inflation rate. Income supplements were an early form of what is now called a Guaranteed Annual Income, a proposal which has been suggested often but never enacted.

The supplements were expensive. Further, new ideologies, such as the population theories of Thomas Malthus and others, proclaimed that the poor were destructive to society and should not be maintained. The English Poor Law Reform Act of 1834 abolished outdoor relief. However it was so harsh and punitive that it never was totally enforced by local officials. The Poor Law Reform Act of 1834 did limit the growth of the public sector in social welfare policy. Further, it stimulated the development of a host of private social welfare efforts, many of which continue today.

The English Poor Laws are important because the values and institutions which they promoted persist with such force today. The distinction, made in 1349 in the Ordinance of Labourers between the able-bodied, undeserving poor, and the non-able-bodied, deserving poor, permeates our present American social policy. For those who are seen as able-bodied, such as single women with children and unemployed youth and men, the major thrust of social policy was and continues to be punitive.

On the other hand, the English Poor Law did establish firmly the responsibility of the community for the non-able-bodied poor. In a market economy, with little or no government interference, it was and remains clear that there are some individuals who have a right to help from the community. This community responsibility is based on early religious teachings, especially the Judeo-Christian ethic, and the practices and philosophies of the early Greeks and Romans. Today there are few who would deny some help to the elderly, the blind, or the disabled poor. The acceptance of this need to provide help is based on these early beliefs, first codified in the Poor Laws of 1349 and 1601.

From the Poor Laws we inherited also the idea of local administration and control. The administration of the Poor Laws was defined in the Law of 1601, and included a federal, county, and local, or parish arrangement, with most control at the parish level. This desire for local control is still strong.

The change from a feudal to a capitalistic or market economy, and the rise of towns and modern industrial methods of production, created severe social and economic dislocations. For the first time, society had to deal with large numbers of unemployed people. Social policy, economic policy, and policy whose purpose was social control all were integrated into the English Poor Laws, which, in many respects, persist today.

NOTES

1. E.M. Leonard, *The Early History of English Poor Law*. London: Frank Cass & Co., Ltd., 1965.

2. Norman Longmate, *The Workhouse*. New York: St. Martin's Press, 1974, p. 14.

3. *Ibid.*

4. Geoffrey W. Oxley, *Poor Relief for England and Wales 1601–1834*. London: David & Charles, 1974.

5. E.M. Leonard, *ibid.*

6. Oxley, *ibid.*, p. 15.

7. Longmate, *ibid.*, p. 17.

8. *Ibid.*, p. 18.

9. James S. Taylor, The Unreformed Workhouse, 1776–1834. In E.W. Martin (ed.). *Comparative Development in Social Welfare*. London: George Allen & Unwin Ltd., 1972, pp. 57–84.

10. Jeffrey Galper, The Speenhamland Scales: Political, Social, or Economic Disaster? *Social Service Review*, March 1970, pp. 54–62.

11. D.A. Baugh, The Cost of Poor Relief in South-East England, 1790–1834. *The Economic History Review*, February, 1975, pp. 50–68.

12. Mark Neuman, Speenhamland in Berkshire. In E.W. Martin (ed.), *Comparative Developments in Social Welfare*, pp. 85–127.

13. Galper, *ibid*, p. 61.

14. D.A. Baugh, *ibid.*, p. 61.

15. *Ibid.*

16. Marque-Luisa Miringoff, The Impact of Population Policy Upon Social Welfare. *Social Service Review*, September 1980, pp. 303–304.

17. Anne Digby, The Labor Market and the Continuity of Social Policy After 1834: The Case of the Eastern Counties. *The Economic History Review*, February 1975, p. 71.

18. Roger Smith, Poor Law and Poor Relief in the 19th Century Midlands. *Midland History* (Vol. 2). 1974, *4*, pp. 216–224.

Chapter 8

SOCIAL POLICY AND FEDERALISM

INTRODUCTION

Major aspects of the English Poor Law were adopted by the United States as it developed a social welfare system. Some of the most important American social policies will be described in this chapter and the following chapters.

A distinctive feature and a continuing issue in American public policy is the distribution of functions, including social welfare functions, among the various levels of government. Because this has been such an important aspect in the development of American public policy, American social policy is described in terms of differing philosophies about the relative powers and functions of the federal, state, and local government.

At the beginning of American history, under Early Federalism, the states retained all powers which were not mentioned explicitly in the Constitution as responsibilities of the federal government. During the Great Depression, it became evident that the federal government and the states needed to work together. As a result, Cooperative Federalism developed. The federal government assumed more power and responsibility. More recently, Presidents Kennedy and Johnson promoted Creative Federalism. Under Creative Federalism, the cities became an important component of public policy, and the federal government became involved in policy areas from which it had been excluded. Under Creative Federalism, beginning efforts were made to decentralize power and responsibility from the federal government to the states and to the localities. This trend was continued by President Nixon and President Reagan under the approach of the New Federalism.

Social welfare policy has been connected intimately with shifts in approaches to intergovernmental relations. This chapter will present an overview of Early Federalism and of Cooperative Federalism. The next chapter will discuss the more contemporary approaches of Creative Federalism and New Federalism.[1]

FORM OF GOVERNMENT AND FEDERAL AND STATE POWER

The way in which the American government is organized has been called federalism. Under American Federalism, the central government shares power and responsibility with the states, and more recently with the cities. Federalism is not the only way to organize government. A more decentralized approach has been called confederation. Before the ratification of the Constitution, there was a confederation—a loose alliance of states. Under the Articles of Confederation, the states had most of the power, and the federal government was relatively weak.

On the other hand, there are governments in which the central authority is very powerful. Other units, such as the states and the cities, derive their power from the central government and are totally dependent on it. This arrangement has been called a unitary form of government. Under a unitary form of government, the central government has the power to change or abolish state and local governments.[2]

The approach of American federalism lies in between the pattern of control in a confederation of states and the pattern in a unitary state. Under the American form of federalism, the state and federal governments share power and responsibility in developing governmental policy and programs. In a broad sense, the various levels of government cooperate with each other.

Table 6 presents the form of government and the relative powers at the federal and state levels.

Table 6: Form of Government and Federal and State Power

Unitary	*Federalism*	*Confederation*
High federal power	Medium federal power	Low federal power
Low state power	Medium state power	High state power

Under federalism, some functions, such as the defense of the country, are accepted as an appropriate responsibility of the federal government. For other functions, such as fire and police protection in a neighborhood, local governments take responsibility. Then there are a large number of functions, such as provisions for social welfare, that began as local responsibilities, became state and local functions, and now are fulfilled by all three levels of government. The central question is, under a system of federalism, which level of government should have what powers and responsibilities in the development and implementation of social policy.

Just as different countries have different approaches to government (whether it is the unitary approach, federalism, or confederation) so, over time, there can be different emphases within an approach. This pattern of changing emphases has been true of American federalism. Figure 2 shows the emphases of the type of federalism and form of government.

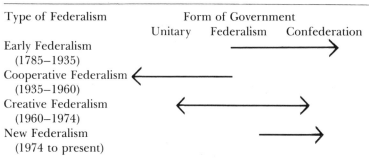

Figure 2: Type of Federalism and Form of Government

Thus under Early Federalism, states' rights were dominant, and the federal government was less powerful. This approach to federalism emphasized the confederation approach. With the national crises created by the Great Depression and the two World Wars, power became more centered in the national government. American federalism drew closer to the unitary form of government.

During the 1960s there were contradictory trends. On the one hand, the federal government became involved in new areas, increasing the unitary approach. On the other hand, efforts were made to decentralize power and decision making to the states and localities. Creative Federalism was the beginning of a trend towards more decentralization. President Nixon's New Federalism reinforced the trend toward diminishing the role of the central government in social policy. New Federalism has been continued and strengthened under President Reagan.

EARLY FEDERALISM

Under Early Federalism, it was felt that the federal government had only those powers which were identified specifically in the Constitution as federal powers. All powers which were not listed as federal powers were seen as the province of the states.

Since the federal government had no formal authority to impose duties on the states, federal grants-in-aid were developed to induce the states to undertake functions deemed by Congress to be in the national interest.[3] The early grants from the federal government to the states were in the form of land and money. Few federal conditions were attached to the grants. Over time, however, the federal government added requirements to the receipt of these grants. If a state was to receive a grant, it had to submit a proposal for approval by the federal government. The agency receiving the grant had to agree to federal specification of the goals and the means in which the grant would be implemented. The recipient, usually a state agency, had to make regular progress reports and allow the federal government to make on-site visits to determine whether the grant was being administered properly. What started out as a relatively free provision of money and land from the federal government to the states assumed a form which enhanced federal control.

The grant-in-aid became known as the conditional grant-in-aid. Under the conditional grant-in-aid, states applied to the federal government for funding. To receive funding, states had to agree to federal goals and means in the implementation of the program. Although they were developed under Early Federalism, conditional grants-in-aid were used more extensively, during the second period, Cooperative Federalism. Conditional grants-in-aid persist today as a major form for the transfer of federal monies to the states and localities for all types of public policy, including social policy. Of all of the types of funding mechanisms, the conditional grants in aid provide the most power and control to the federal government. Resistance to federal power and control is a major reason that the conditional grants-in-aid are opposed by some today.

EARLY AMERICAN SOCIAL WELFARE PROVISIONS

Under Early Federalism, most social welfare services were provided by the state and local governments and by the private sector. Originally, provision of help for those in need in Colonial America followed English Poor Law approaches. The deserving poor who could live in their own homes were provided with outdoor relief. Abled-bodied children and adults were apprenticed to farmers and businessmen. Individuals who were not self-sufficient, such as the severely emotionally ill and the disabled, were placed in private homes at government expense, and later, in public institutions called almshouses. Local government had major responsibility for the provision of social welfare services, which started as early as 1642 in the Plymouth Colony. During Colonial times, help to those in need was relatively generous. As

Walter Trattner writes, "most communities attacked the problem of poverty with a high degree of civic responsibility."[4]

The American Revolution caused social and economic dislocations and resulted in the disruption of many community administered social policies. During the late seventeenth century and early eighteenth century, the number of poor people in America had grown significantly. In addition, classical economists and population theorists in Europe were attacking social welfare approaches. They felt that providing too much help for the poor would lead to a population of poor citizens too large for society's resources. The dependency of the poor would inhibit society's progress.

As communities grew larger and more impersonal, it became more difficult to take care of the poor, the handicapped, and the mentally ill by having them live in private homes. There was a trend towards building almshouses to take care of those in need.

While there were other types of relief, the almshouse became the most widely used. The almshouse sheltered the old, the young, the sick, the poor, the emotionally ill, the blind, the addicted, and the criminal. Children still were apprenticed to businessmen or farmers. Some needy people avoided the almshouse and received public outdoor relief. However, relief was kept at subsistence levels. The names of the recipients were placed on a pauper roll that often was reproduced in the newspapers.[5]

In an effort to overcome some of the worst aspects of the almshouse, reformers started pressing for more specialized institutions. Thomas Gallaudet was able to get support for an institution, founded in 1819, for the deaf. Another strong and effective crusader was Dorothea Dix. She established many state institutions for the mentally ill. During the middle 1800s there were state institutions established for the blind and for juvenile delinquents. As the result of reform efforts, these institutions tended to avoid some of the worst aspects of the almshouses. Still, many institutions, especially those for the mentally ill, became expensive and often fell into a state of neglect. Contemporary reformers have worked to close many of the institutions established in the nineteenth century. They have felt that the mentally ill and the retarded could be helped more effectively and more efficiently in their home communities.

With a few exceptions, including Federal help for the veterans of the Revolutionary War,[6] the federal government generally did not participate in social welfare efforts during Early Federalism. There was a general consensus in the country that social welfare was the responsibility of the states and the localities and of private charity. The Supreme Court interpreted the constitutional phase, that the federal government has the power to "promote the general welfare, " extremely narrowly. The Supreme Court felt that this phrase excluded the federal government from social welfare, even from protecting women and children who were abused in the workplace. The executive branch shared this philosophy. In a famous decision, President Pierce vetoed a bill, inspired by Dorothea Dix, that would have granted the states federal land for poor emotionally ill individuals. President Pierce argued that if this bill became law, Congress would be able to provide assistance for all poor persons and thus transfer what had been a state and local responsibility to the federal government.[7] The president wrote, ". . . I cannot find any authority in the Constitution for making the Federal Government the greater almoner (provider) of public charity throughout the United States."[8]

During the beginning of Early Federalism, the powers of the federal government and the states were separate and more or less equal. As Jane Clark described Early Federalism ". . . viewed from a distance, the landscape of government in the United States appeared to contain two separate federal and state streams flowing in distinct but closely parallel channels."[9]

PRIVATE CHARITY

Toward the end of the 1800s private social agencies assumed major social welfare responsibilities. To help individuals, Charity Organization Societies were developed. The first was organized in London in 1869 under the title, The Society for Organizing Charitable Relief and Repressing Mendicity.

In general, the Charity Organization Societies were based

on individualist philosophy. The early Charity Organization Societies tended to blame individuals for their problems and tried to force them to adjust to the existing system. They provided money and goods to needy persons, but only after a careful determination of need and under strict conditions. Careful records were kept and efforts were made to standardize the help which was given. The Charity Organization Societies were the beginning of a movement to transform the provision of moral encouragement and advice to a systematic group of professional skills.[10]

The Charity Organization Societies were the predecessors of our modern family service agencies. Originally, they used volunteers to help people in need. The private charity movement grew during the late 1800s. For example, in Philadelphia by 1878, there were over 800 private charity and church groups which helped the poor by raising more than $1.5 million annually.

An early leader of the Charity Organization movement was Mary Richmond, who published the first casework book, *Social Diagnosis,* in 1917. She believed that the scientific method of study, diagnosis, and treatment could be applied to the treatment of individuals. For Mary Richmond, knowledge of human behavior was essential to appropriate help. She also stressed the utilization of community resources and a democratic process in which the worker and the client cooperated.[11]

The need for consistent training of the volunteers who worked for the Charity Organization Societies became evident. The first school of social work was established in the summer of 1898. By 1904, a 1 year curriculum was developed under the name of the New York School of Philanthropy. In 1912, a 2 year graduate program was started. This program was the predecessor of the Columbia University School of Social Work.

A different approach was taken by the Settlement House Movement, also supported by private funds. Toynbee Hall in London, England, was the first settlement house. It was established in 1884 when two English university students moved into, or settled, in a building in a low-income London neighborhood. Originally, the settlement's purpose was to bring culture, such as great art and music, to the poor in order to raise their moral standard. In addition, it was felt that the settlement house could spread healthy, rural values, to combat the immoral influences of the city.

The settlement house idea spread to the growing American cities. As social conditions became more fully understood, the philosophy changed. In contrast to the individualism of the Charity Organization Societies, the Settlement House promoted a more collectivist philosophy. Early leaders, such as Jane Adams at Hull House, believed that social conditions needed to be changed and that government should intervene in society to help those in need. Settlement House workers were active in the progressive efforts of the day. They worked for the protection of women and children on the job, in the early union and civil rights movement, in efforts to get the vote for women, and in efforts to improve low income communities.

The typical settlement house worker was a single young adult. The settlement house workers lived in the communities they were helping. These communities usually were composed of working class immigrants. By living with and working daily with those in need, they developed an understanding of poverty and a commitment to change social conditions. Many of the settlement house workers went on to important positions in government at all levels. An example is Harry Hopkins, who helped to develop and administer the New Deal for President Franklin Roosevelt.

The early settlement house workers were called social workers. They brought to the profession a basic commitment to change inequitable social conditions.[12]

COOPERATIVE FEDERALISM

Over time there was a gradual and steady increase in federal power. This increase was reflected in federal conditional grant-in-aid legislation and by the actions of the executive branch of government in the administration of grants. In social welfare, incomplete and uncoordinated efforts by private charities were supplemented by government, first at the local level and then at the state level. Taken as a whole, these efforts were clearly inadequate, and federal help was needed. Resistance to federal intervention in social welfare was overcome by the crisis created by the Great Depression of 1929. In addition, the Great Depression required that the federal and state governments work more closely together than they had in the past. This new relationship between the federal and state government has been called Cooperative Federalism.

Scholars disagree about when Cooperative Federalism began. Some, like Morton Grodzins, believe that elements of Cooperative Federalism have existed since the beginning of the country and became dominant after 1935.[13] Others identify as the beginning of Cooperative Federalism programs developed in response to the problems created by the Great Depression, because they see these programs as totally different from those programs of Early Federalism.

Michael Reagen writes that under Cooperative Federalism, ". . . the national and state governments work together in the same areas, sharing functions and therefore power."[14] There is cooperation in operating programs. In contrast to Early Federalism, the emphasis is less on the legal and constitutional positions of the levels of governments. Instead, there are "intergovernmental relations" based on practical working relationships. Since there has been a resistance to federal operation of local programs, there has been a ". . . compromise of shared functions, permitting both national stimulation and financing and state and local operation of programs to take necessary variations in application into account."[15]

Compared to earlier approaches, Cooperative Federalism in operation meant an increase of federal power. The emphasis in federalism tended more toward the unitary approach. In a series of decisions, the Supreme Court rejected the interpretation that the federal government was confined to the powers mentioned specifically in the Constitution, while all other powers reverted to the states.[16]

EARLY SOCIAL WELFARE PROGRAMS DURING COOPERATIVE FEDERALISM

A new approach to the role and responsibility of government in relation to the economy and to those in need began around 1900. According to Richard Hofstadter, "the relatively untrammeled capitalism of the nineteenth century was beginning to change into the welfare capitalism of the twentieth; the frustrations of the middle class and the needs of the poor were accelerating the change. Men sensed that a different order was slowly arising."[17]

At the beginning of the twentieth century, middle class citizens started to fear the large private business and financial empires being created by individuals such as Henry Ford, Andrew Carnegie, John D. Rockefeller, and Andrew W. Mellon. Middle class Americans worried that their status and standard of living could disappear. "In a society of great collective aggregates, the traditional emphasis upon the exploits of the individual lost much of its appeal."[18] The progressive movement captured the attention and support of the fearful middle class.

With its campaign for a wide range of reforms, the Progressive movement laid the groundwork for later expansions of governmental authority. As Robert Bremner writes:

> Nearly all of these reforms involved limitations on private property rights and extension of public authority into areas previously regarded as the exclusive preserve of individual initiative. Taken one by one, the proposals were neither novel nor drastic. Collectively, however, they implied that a new attitude toward politics and economics was taking shape. They demonstrated a strong tendency to substitute public benefit for private profit as the measure of industrial efficiency.[19]

Before the passage of the Social Security Bill in 1935, the federal government had developed some relatively small welfare related efforts. For example, the Bureau of Refugees, Freedmen, and Abandoned Lands (Freedman's Bureau) was created within the War Department in 1865 to help newly freed slaves.[20] In 1912, the Children's Bureau was established within the Department of Labor to investigate and report on all matters related to the welfare of children.[21] The Sheppard-Towner Act was passed in 1921, after 3 years of bitter conflict. The Sheppard-Towner Act, also known as the Infancy and Maternity Act, established 3,000 child and maternal health centers in 45 states.

Walter Trattner writes, "On the statute to provide federal grants-in-aid to the states for a welfare program other than education were reared many of the cooperative federal–state programs established under the Social Security Act of 1935.[22]

The Vocational Rehabilitation Act of 1920 provided federal help, to be matched by the states, for disabled veterans. The Vocational Rehabilitation Act was strongly opposed by state and local public health officials who felt that it was an infringement on their authority.[23]

FEDERAL SOCIAL WELFARE PROGRAMS DURING THE GREAT DEPRESSION

The Depression of the 1930s found America unprepared to deal with the problems of economic insecurity typical of a modern, industrial society. While workmen's compensation was widespread, it was generally inadequate. All but four states had workmen's compensation laws by 1930. However, in 12 of these states, coverage applied only to hazardous occupations. In many of the other states, the worker bore 50 to 80 percent of the cost.[24]

Many states had been providing some form of public assistance before passage of the Social Security Act of 1935. The first law on a state level that provided aid for dependent children was passed in 1911. The first old age assistance law was passed in 1914. By 1934, 27 states had some form of old age assistance, 45 states had some form of state aid to dependent children, and 27 states had some form of aid to the needy blind. Many of these state laws consisted primarily of enabling legislation to permit local jurisdictions to fund and administer these services. In 1934, there were approximately 180,000 recipients of some form of old age assistance. Approximately 280,000 dependent children were receiving aid.

The growing economic depression placed increasing pressures on local and state welfare systems. The crisis changed drastically people's attitudes about federal government. As Gaston Rimlinger writes, "The expectation now was that the government somehow had to take charge of the economy; it had to become responsible for the general performance of the system."[25] The local and state welfare systems and the private insurance companies had been unable to meet a clear, pressing, and national need. Specific federal intervention was all that was left.

The federal government first became involved in the area of emergency relief in 1932 with the establishment of the Reconstruction Finance Corporation (RFC). The RFC was authorized to make loans up to $300 million to states and localities to relieve destitution. Later the law was changed to read that the loans did not have to be repaid. The RFC became a grant-in-aid type program.

The Federal Emergency Relief Administration (FERA) was established in 1933. It represented the largest short-run program in the history of grants-in-aid. Between 1933 and 1936, FERA made grants-in-aid of $3 billion to the states. Approximately two-thirds of this total was spent in 1935. The grants were used for work relief and direct relief, although the federal government favored the former. Direct relief was made in cash or in kind to those who were unemployed. FERA was different from previous grant-in-aid programs in that federal administrators were given almost complete discretion in the allocation of federal aid. Ultimately, federal administrators had the power to take over and administer a state program if it was not being operated properly.

The Civil Works Administration (CWA) operated concurrently with FERA. In about three months during the end of 1933 and the beginning of 1934, CWA spent almost $1 billion. Through the CWA, state Public Welfare agencies became agencies of the federal government. The federal government paid directly workers who were on CWA projects.

The Works Progress Administration, later called the Works Projects Administration (WPA), was established in 1935 to replace FERA. The WPA developed and administered a new work relief program for all unemployed workers. It was a federal program. The national government determined the policy and administered the program, with some state and local government participation. During its existence, WPA spent over $10 billion in federal funds, the largest amount spent so far for any single relief program. In addition, the administrator of WPA was given "more extensive authority with respect to the distribution of public funds and the control of local activities than any other governmental officer in time of peace."[26]

The Federal Emergency Administration of Public Works was established in 1933. Later known as the Public Works Administration (PWA), it created public works programs. PWA provided both grants and loans. ". . . The Public Works Administration broke with all earlier grants-in-aid precedents by establishing direct federal-local relationships with reference to the states."[27]

On August 14, 1935, the Social Security Act was approved and became law. It has been called, ". . . one of the major events in the history of federal grants-in-aid."[28] The original bill provided for a nationally administered old age insurance system, which we now know as Social Security. Compulsory contributions from employees and employers in covered occupations financed the insurance system. Under the Social Security Act, states also were encouraged to establish and administer unemployment compensation programs. Federal monies were available to operate these programs under the public assistance provision.

The original Social Security bill provided federal grants-in-aid to states for the needy aged and blind and for families with dependent children. More recently, aid to the blind, the elderly poor, and the disabled has become part of the federally administered Social Security System. The state and/or county administered public assistance programs serve families with dependent children. Public assistance funding comes from both federal and state monies.

Among other provisions, the Social Security Act required states to make programs available in all political subdivisions and established federal minimum standards for eligibility. Within broad limits, the states were free to establish the scope of their public assistance programs. "The enactment by Congress in 1935 of a broad Social Security program, based on the grant-in-aid device, resulted in an increase in 1937 to the highest level of regular grant expenditures yet reached, and also laid the groundwork for future increases."[29]

SUMMARY

A major issue in social policy is the relative powers and responsibilities of the federal, state, and local government in the delivery of social programs. Historically, intergovernmental relations in social policy have followed national attitudes about federalism. During Early Federalism, when states' rights were emphasized, most social welfare programs were delivered by the states and the localities and by the private charities. As the country grew, it became evident that a more active federal role was needed in public policy. To facilitate this role, the conditional grant-in-aid was developed. Under the conditional grant-in-aid, state and local governments apply for and receive grants and agree to federally specified goals and means.

During Cooperative Federalism, there was greater federal participation and control in social policy than there had been under Early Federalism. The Great Depression created the need for a series of federal programs. With the passage of the Social Security Act in 1935, the principle of federal involvement in social policy to improve the general welfare was established finally and firmly.

From Early Federalism, where for the most part, all powers not explicitly provided to the federal government were reserved to the states, through Cooperative Federalism, where the federal government, along with the states, had the power to provide for the general welfare, there had been a dramatic increase in federal power vis-a-vis the states and localities. While this trend was to continue, at the same time, beginning pressures toward decentralization and local coordination culminated ultimately in a new pattern of federal-state relationships—first Creative Federalism and then New Federalism. In the dramatic growth of federal power were the seeds of decentralization.

NOTES

1. These chapters are based on Robert Magill, *Community Decision Making for Social Welfare: Federalism, City Government, and the Poor.* New York: Human Sciences Press, 1979.

2. Claudius Johnson, H. Paul Castleberry, Daniel M. Ogden, Jr., & Thor Swanson. *American National Government,* (5th ed.). New York: Thomas Y. Crowell, 1960, p. 124.

3. V.O. Key, *The Administration of Federal Grants to the States.* Chicago: Public Administration Service, 1937, p. 4.

4. Walter I. Trattner, *From Poor Law to Welfare State: A History of Social Welfare in America.* New York: The Free Press, 1974, pp. 15–27.

5. Kathleen Woodroofe, *From Charity to Social Work in England and the United States.* Toronto: University of Toronto Press, 1962, p. 84.

6. John P. Resch, Federal Welfare for Revolutionary War Veterans. *Social Service Review,* June 1982, pp. 171–195.

7. Extract from *Congressional Globe.* Thirty-Third Congress, 1st Session, May 3, 1854, pp. 1061–1063. Reprinted in S. P. Breckinridge, Public Welfare Administration in the United States: Selected Documents. Chicago: University of Chicago Press, 1938. Reprinted in Fran Breul & Alan Wade, *Readings in Social Welfare Policy,* University of Chicago, School of Social Service Administration, III-D1.

8. *Ibid.,* p. 111-D2.

9. Jane Clark, *The Rise of a New Federalism: Federal-State Cooperation in the United States.* New York: Columbia University Press, 1938, p. 8.

10. Gerald Handel, *Social Welfare in Western Society.* New York: Random House, 1982, pp. 214–215.

11. Kathleen Woodroofe, *From Charity to Social Work in England and the United States.* Toronto: University of Toronto Press, 1962.

12. Allen F. Davis, *Spearheads for Reform: The Social Settlements and the Progressive Movement 1890–1914.* New York: Oxford University Press, 1974.

13. Grodzins, Morton, In Daniel J. Elazar. (ed.), *The American System: A New View of Government in the United States.* Chicago: Rand McNally, 1966, pp. 51–59.

14. Reagen, Michael D. *The New Federalism.* New York: Oxford University Press, 1972, pp. 20–21.

15. *Ibid.,* pp. 22–23.

16. Magill, *ibid.,* pp. 60–62.

17. Richard Hofstadter, *Social Darwinsim in American Thought*. Boston: Beacon Press, 1955, p. 119.

18. *Ibid.*, p. 119.

19. Robert Bremner, *From the Depths: The Discovery of Poverty in the United States*. New York: New York University Press, 1960, p. 138.

20. Victoria Olds, The Freedmen's Bureau: A Nineteenth-Century Federal Welfare Agency. *Social Casework*, May 1963, *44,* 251–252.

21. Blanche D. Coll, *Perspectives in Public Welfare: A History.* Washington, D.C.: U.S. Government Printing Office, U.S. Department of Health, Education and Welfare, Social and Rehabilitation Service, Office of Research, Demonstrations and Training, Intramural Division, 1969, pp. 73–74.

22. Walter Trattner, *From Poor Law to Welfare State: A History of Social Welfare in America*. New York: The Free Press, 1974, pp. 185–186.

23. Earl M. Baker, Bernadette A. Stevens, Stephen L. Schecter, & Harlan A. Wright, *Federal Grants, The National Interest and State Response: A Review of Theory and Research*. Philadelphia: Temple University, Center for the Study of Federalism, p. 28.

24. Bureau of Labor Statistics, *Handbook of Labor Statistics*, 1931, published as Bulletin No. 541. Washington, D.C.: U.S. Government Printing Office, 1931, p. 479.

25. Gaston Rimlinger, *Welfare Policy and Industrialization in Europe, America and Russia*. New York: John Wiley & Sons, 1971, p. 199.

26. Committee on Federal Grants-in-Aid, Council of State Governments, *Federal Grants-in-Aid*. Washington, D.C.: The Council of State Governments, 1949, p. 175.

27. *Ibid.*, pp. 175–176.

28. *Ibid.*, p. 148.

29. *Ibid.*, p. 34.

Chapter 9

FEDERALISM DURING THE PAST TWO DECADES—CREATIVE FEDERALISM AND NEW FEDERALISM

INTRODUCTION

The 1960s were a period of ferment and change. Serious domestic problems had received little federal attention during the presidency of Dwight Eisenhower. Frustration over the lack of government response to racial segregation and poverty led to civil rights marches and destructive urban riots. Government finally responded to this upheaval with the most significant advances in social policy since the Great Depression. On a structural level, a new approach to the relationship between the federal government, the states, and the cities was developed. It has been called Creative Federalism.

Creative Federalism combined aspects of both the unitary and the confederation approaches to government. On the one hand, the federal government became involved in areas which previously had been state and local functions. Expansions of federal power occurred in the areas of civil rights and voting rights. New federal programs were developed in the areas of poverty, physical health, mental health, education, and job training.

On the other hand, many policy makers felt that too much power was concentrated in the federal government. The proliferation of conditional grants-in-aid was creating confusion and inefficiency. In reaction, the federal government during Creative Federalism, returned some power and decision making to states and localities. This trend was to be accelerated during the 1970s under the New Federalism.

SOCIAL PROBLEMS WHICH LED TO CREATIVE FEDERALISM

The deteriorating condition of the cities was one of the nation's major domestic problems during the 1950s. The cities had been a long-neglected part of the federal system. Cities are creatures of the states and are legally dependent on states. The Iowa Supreme Court ruled in 1863 that "municipal corporations owe their origin to, and derive their powers and rights wholly from, the legislature . . . It may destroy, it may abridge and control municipalities . . . ."[1] This decision is known as Dillion's rule, after the Iowa Supreme Court Justice who wrote it. Dillion's rule defined the legal status of cities. Under it, cities are dependent on the states. However, given the strong tradition of local self rule, states have granted cities the right of home rule, or the right to govern their own affairs.

Since 1920, the urban population had exceeded the rural population, and federal payments to the cities had been increasing since 1932.[2] However, the major relationship in the federal system had been between the national government and the states. In the early 1960s, recognizing the problems of the cities, ". . . Congress for the first time authorized aid to local communities for a virtually unrestricted range of functions . . ."[3]

During the 1950s, the country experienced sluggish economic growth, a rise in unemployment, problems related to automation and migration to the cities, and a new awareness of the problem of racial inequality. In 1953, unemployment was 20 percent higher among Blacks than among whites. Between 1953 and 1963, the average differential rose to 112 percent.

Since the middle of the twentieth century, there had been a

migration of poor Blacks from the South to Northern, Midwestern, and Western cities. Between 1950 and 1960, 1,400,000 Blacks left the South. This movement resulted partly from the mechanization of Southern agriculture. The influx placed serious pressure on the economies and public welfare systems of these cities.[4] Yet little attention was paid to these problems by the administration of Dwight Eisenhower.

In the 1960s, the country was in the midst of the Civil Rights Movement. The Civil Rights Movement exerted strong pressure on all levels of society to respond to the needs of minorities. One consequence of the Civil Rights Movement was an increase in voting by minorities. Some feel that President Kennedy owed his slim victory over Richard Nixon in the 1960 presidential election to the votes of minorities, especially Blacks.

The approach toward government was also different in the 1960s. John Kennedy and Lyndon Johnson were elected as activist presidents. It was becoming increasingly clear that the social and economic integration of minority persons into American society could be accomplished only by federal action. After the relative quiet of the 1950s, much of the country was ready for the federal government to deal directly with urgent domestic problems. In addition, at the beginning of the 1960s, the country was in a period of prosperity. There was a federal budget surplus which would be used for new domestic programs.

CREATIVE FEDERALISM

Creative Federalism involved a new approach to intergovernmental relationships. In part, Creative Federalism was an expansion of federal power and responsibility into new functions, primarily in the areas of social policy. However, at the same time, there were efforts to decentralize power and decision making in order to give states, localities, and citizens more control.

Many leaders were concerned about the accumulation of power in Washington. John Gardner, a Secretary of the Department of Health, Education and Welfare, was fearful that the federal government was overpowering the states and localities.

He wrote, "We must revitalize the state and local leadership so that it can play its role vis-a-vis an increasingly powerful federal government; we must revitalize . . . so they can play a vital role in the partnerships without being completely submerged and obliterated."[5] One way to achieve this objective was to restrict the development of specific grants-in-aid. Many felt that local leadership and competence would develop if the localities were not always dependent on the federal governments.[6]

Decentralization began to be stressed in a different way; it was understood as the dispersion of power to the people. As Richard Goodwin, a close advisor to President Kennedy, wrote, the goal ". . . must be to meet specific ills through methods which can in themselves enlarge the sense and reality of individual relevance and participation . . . Both burden and enterprise must be shifted into units of action small enough to widen the outlets for direct participation and control."[7]

As a result of these concerns, most of the policies under Creative Federalism provided for citizen participation. Many policies established community based social planning mechanisms. The Community Action Section of the Poverty Program was perhaps the most well known for its requirement that there be "maximum feasible participation" by the recipients of services.

Another aspect of Creative Federalism was direct city-federal governmental relationships. In the past, federal programs for urban areas typically were controlled by state government. These governments, often dominated by rural and suburban interests, tended to be insensitive to urban needs. In a significant new approach to solve domestic social problems, Creative Federalism included cities as a part of federalism.

To accomplish these changes, greater reliance was placed on the block grant. The block grant resembles the conditional grant-in-aid in two of its features. Under both the block grant and the conditional grant-in-aid, states and localities take the initiative in applying for funds. The federal government establishes the policy goals under both the conditional grant-in-aid and the block grant. The block grant differs from the conditional grant-in-aid in that the block grant gives states and localities the freedom to select the means, the specific programs, to implement the federally developed goals. In contrast to the conditional grant-in-aid, the block grant provides states and localities with more decision making authority. Introduced in the 1960s, the block grant form persists today.

In summary, the major aspects of Creative Federalism were:

Significant expansion of the federal government into new functions, primarily through expanded social policies,

Inclusion of cities as a major part of American federalism and the initiation of extensive direct federal-city intergovernmental relations,

Decentralization of some power and decision making from the federal government to the states and localities through provisions for more state and local planning and through citizen and public official participation in policy decision making, and

Reliance upon the block grant to transfer money from the federal government to the states and the localities. The block grant provides for federally established goals, but in contrast to the conditional grant-in-aid, the block grant ensures state and local involvement in the selection of means, or programs, to accomplish these goals.

While Creative Federalism increased the federal government's role in social policy, it began a process of giving state and local governments more control over the way public policy was implemented. This trend has continued under the most recent approach to intergovernmental relations, New Federalism.

SOCIAL WELFARE PROGRAMS DURING CREATIVE FEDERALISM

During Creative Federalism, there was an expansion of social policy unequaled since the Great Depression. During both periods, there were serious threats to social, economic, and political stability. Just as it did during the depression the federal government responded in the 1960s by developing new social policies. For example, the Poverty Program provided social services, jobs, and training to residents of low income neighborhoods. The Civil Rights Act of 1964 prohibited discrimination on the basis of race, sex, or ethnic group in employment. The Voting Rights Act insured the right to vote to minorities who in many communities had been denied this basic right. The Food Stamp Act was an improvement over the existing program of distribution of specific surplus commodities to the poor. The Food Stamp program was important in significantly reducing starvation and inadequate nutrition.

In the area of health care, significant advances were made. Medicare and Medicaid were established in 1965. Medicare provided many hospital and medical care benefits for the elderly with payment primarily by the federal government. Medicaid, a federal and state program, provided some medical services for the poor in participating states.

The Community Mental Health Act provided decentralized mental health programs in communities and was important in the deinstitutionalization of many of the mentally disabled.

Other programs for social change were introduced and flourished. Social policies were developed to improve social services in public welfare. Rational planning approaches to improve the economy of distressed regions of the country were authorized in the Area Redevelopment Act of 1961 and the Economic Redevelopment Act of 1965. In the Model Cities Program, advanced social planning methods were directed towards the comprehensive social, physical, and economic renewal of inner city neighborhoods. The Elementary and Secondary Education Act provided additional educational opportunities and social services to disadvantaged children and their families. For the unemployed, a number of job and training programs were developed to create new employment opportunities.[8]

These and other social policies represented a massive effort to improve the condition of people in need in American society.

They provided dramatic results. Poverty was reduced. Participation was broadened in political activities. Mental health, physical health, education, and housng were improved for those most in need.

These improvements were accompanied by an increase in the size of government and the taxes needed to pay for it. In addition, as the country became more involved in the Vietnam War, it became more difficult to have both "guns and butter." Social welfare programs began to suffer as more money was needed to support the military buildup.

The Creative Federalism of Lyndon Johnson and John Kennedy was a first step in consolidating the proliferating grants of earlier administrations. More community decision making and planning, direct federal–city funding of programs, and participation of those affected by the programs were the hallmarks of many of the newer programs.

The goals of Creative Federalism were, on the one hand, to consolidate, coordinate, and rationalize the mammoth federal grant-in-aid structure. A second purpose was decentralization, both to lower levels of government and to the people themselves. The growing power and influence of Washington had to be limited.

Creative Federalism was a reaction against the past. Cooperative Federalism had resulted in greater federal power. Creative Federalism began to limit some of this power. But for some, Creative Federalism did not go far enough in returning power to the local communities. It was up to the Republicans to press this goal under the New Federalism.

THE NEW FEDERALISM

President Richard Nixon pursued the decentralization started under Creative Federalism. Basic to Nixon's New Federalism was returning power and decision making authority in the area of domestic policy to the state and community level. In terms of governmental form, the New Federalism was actually an attempt to return to Early Federalism, with its emphasis on states' rights and confederation. This trend has continued and been expanded by President Reagan.

Nixon was hostile toward social welfare. During his administration, a major effort was made to dismantle the Poverty Program. Nixon deliberately destroyed the Model Cities Program by merging it into a new block grant in the area of housing and urban development. His effort to decentralize decision making through the new General Revenue Sharing Program was consistent with his hostility to social welfare, because social welfare interests generally have the least support on the community level.

General Revenue Sharing was first enacted in 1972 as the State and Local Assistance Act. Under General Revenue Sharing, federally collected monies are distributed to states, counties, and cities. There is almost no federal control over the goals or the means. Cities can use General Revenue Sharing money for police protection, parks and recreation, health, social welfare, education, pollution control, fire protection, and general administration of the city. The money comes to state and local government automatically, based on a formula. State and local governments do not need to develop detailed proposals which could be changed or rejected by the federal government.

Richard Nathan has suggested the following rationale as the most frequently cited justification for adopting General Revenue Sharing:

> To help meet domestic public needs at the state and local level,
>
> To stabilize or reduce state and local taxes, particularly the property tax,
>
> To decentralize government,
>
> To equalize fiscal conditions between rich and poor states and rich and poor localities,
>
> To alter the nation's overall tax system by placing greater reliance on income taxation (predominantly federal) as opposed to property and sales taxation.[9]

In addition, it was felt that General Revenue Sharing would reduce the size and importance of the federal conditional grant-in-aid program. In fact, during the first years of operation, General Revenue Sharing accounted for almost 25 percent of the total federal grants to state and local government.[10]

General Revenue Sharing completes the philosophical return to state and local control characteristic of this country's early confederation approach to intergovernmental relations. At present, General Revenue Sharing represents a small amount of the total federal monies which still are provided, to states and localities. Conditional grants-in-aid and block grants still are the conduits for most of the money received from the Federal government.

The experience of General Revenue Sharing is not encouraging to those who both support social welfare and want more state and local control. When cities were totally free to choose where to use their funds, only 2 percent were allocated and spent on projects identified as social services for the poor and aged. Further, as could be expected, a study of the actual spending of Revenue Sharing money indicated that the category of local administration increased the most.[11] When there is complete local control, the mayor and city bureaucrats expand their bureaucracy. It can be assumed that many of the appointments are political appointments which take precedence over specific policy needs of the city.[12]

Further, social service allocations under General Revenue Sharing are related directly to interest group pressure and inversely related to measures of need, such as percent unemployed. An impirical study of social service allocations in 22 randomly selected American communities showed that decentralization under General Revenue Sharing resulted in social policies which were responsive to interest group pressures but unresponsive to need.

During the first two years of the program, cities which spent relatively high percentages of their General Revenue Sharing monies for social services had low rates of unemployment but relatively active interest groups pressing for monies for the poor and aged. Cities which allocated a smaller percentage of their General Revenue Sharing monies for social services for the poor and aged had higher rates of unemployment, but less active interest groups working for support of the poor and aged. In contrast, when outside controls were placed on social welfare grants, as in the Community Action Program allocations, social policy tended to be more responsive to community need.[13]

The trend toward increased local control was viewed with suspicion by many concerned with social welfare services. Writing about General Revenue Sharing in the summer of 1972, several months before its passage, Gerald Wheeler observed that "Localism has consistently worked against the poor and minority groups. If undue power is concentrated in Washington, it has become so as the only feasible alternative available in the attempt to secure membership of America's disadvantaged and disenfranchised groups in the larger society. . . . If the destiny of Americans . . . is transferred to state and local governments, the end result will be to turn back history with respect to human welfare."[14]

A similar position was put forth by Wilbur Cohen, a past Secretary of the U.S. Department of Health, Education, and Welfare. Cohen wrote, "We have to have federal programs with strings attached because it is the only way that the disadvantaged, the poor whites and poor blacks will get their fair share. If there are not federally regulated programs to disburse money and instead it is handled by local city governments, then they won't get their fair share."[15]

The Presidency of Ronald Reagan has furthered the New Federalism. Massive budget cuts in the area of social welfare have been accompanied by efforts towards less federal control and more state and local control. Conditional grants-in-aid have been merged into block grants. These new block grants are in the areas of maternal and child health, primary health, preventive health services, alcohol, drug abuse and mental health, community services, social services, education, and energy assistance. The immediate results have been disastrous for social welfare clients and their workers.

A major consequence of this return to the philosophy of

Early Federalism is that the role of the federal government in supporting social justice is being curtailed greatly. A continuation of this trend will result in greater social and economic inequality in American society.

TAXES AND SOCIAL POLICY

General Revenue Sharing is a very popular program with state and local officials, because it gives them total control in program development. In addition, General Revenue Sharing provides new resources to operate state and local government. Since the 1900s there has been a dramatic shift of resources away from local government and towards state and the federal government. To some extent, this shift has occurred because of the types of taxes which are associated with the different levels of government.

In 1913 the national government instituted the federal income tax. Under the income tax, as people make more money, both in real and in inflated dollars, they are pushed into higher tax brackets. This bracket creep means that as an individual's salary increases, a greater percentage goes to the federal government in the form of income taxes. Economists call the income tax an elastic tax because the federal share increases as peoples' salaries increase. Without legislating new taxes, the federal government increases its income with even a moderate rate of inflation. At this writing, bracket creep may not continue because of a new law which indexes an individual's income to the rate of inflation.

On the other hand, cities raise most of their money through the property tax. This tax is a relatively inelastic tax, because it usually does not keep up with inflation. The lag occurs in part because property values are not assessed every year. When housing values rise, as they generally have during this century, cities do not receive more money automatically. The effect over time of the elasticity of the income tax and the inelasticity of the property tax has been an increase in the federal treasury and a relative decline in monies raised by localities.

At the same time, more and more services are being demanded of city governments. The result is that there has been a steady increase in federal support of various city functions, through conditional grants-in-aid, block grants, and General Revenue Sharing. It is not unusual, at present, for over half of a city's operating budget to be made up of federal monies, which supplement the property tax.

General Revenue Sharing was not seen only as a way to decentralize power and authority. It was also a mechanism for helping many cities on the brink of bankruptcy by providing, in effect, a limited income tax for them. In other words, if monies collected through the federal income tax are returned with no conditions to the cities, the cities are being given a small percentage of the federal income tax.

The distributional effects of various types of taxes also are related directly to federal, state, and local relationships. The income tax is the most progressive of the taxes. Progressive taxation means that, to some extent, the higher an income, the greater is the percentage of that income vulnerable to the tax. Low income people pay a lower percentage of their income to the Internal Revenue Service than do high income people.

On the other hand, the property tax can be a regressive tax. Regressive taxation means that low income persons pay a higher percentage of their income to taxes than do high income persons. Certainly, a family of four with an annual income of $15,000 is going to pay a higher percentage of its income for property taxes than will a family of four whose annual income is $150,000, even though the second family might pay more in dollar amounts.

Other taxes, including the sales tax, usually a state tax, and the Social Security tax, tend to be regressive also. Since low and middle income people tend to spend more of their income than do high income people, more of their income is vulnerable to the sales tax. If a rich person invests half of his or her income, only 50 percent of that income is available for the sales tax. A poorer person who spends almost all of his or her income for goods and services might have 85 to 90 percent vulnerable to the sales tax. Similarly, the Social Security tax, which taxes income

up to a certain level, is a regressive tax for low and middle income people. All of low and middle income earnings are vulnerable to the tax, while upper income persons pay Social Security
taxes on only a percentage of their earnings.

There are important implications for the relationships between the federal, state, and local governments in the types of
taxes they levy and the distributional effects of these taxes. To
the extent that federal monies are withdrawn from social policies which then are to be supported at the local level, the property tax will be substituted for the income tax. The property tax
tends to be both a regressive tax, and one which does not respond quickly to inflation. Of all the taxes, the property tax is
least suited to support huge social welfare programs.

Even though the income tax is moderately progressive, it is
a very unpopular tax. Its unpopularity comes in part from its
visibility. At one time during the year, individuals see how much
they pay for income tax. The same visibility is true of the property tax. On the other hand, the sales tax is a less visible tax. Most
people would be shocked to see how much they pay in sales tax
during a year. However, few people ever know the total they pay
in sales tax. Even though the sales tax is a regressive tax, hurting
low and middle income people the most, it is not as unpopular as
the income tax and the property tax. Because of this relative
invisibility, some countries, like Sweden, make major use of a
national sales tax, called a Value Added Tax, along with a very
progressive income tax, to support their extensive social welfare
system.

SUMMARY

During the 1960s there was a dramatic increase in social
policy sponsored by the federal government. At the same time,
efforts were made to strengthen state and local control in the
implementation of these policies. Major advances in coping with
social problems were accomplished. The country dramatically
reduced the percentage of families in poverty. Minorities participated more fully in public affairs, and riots and civil disruption

almost were eliminated. Dramatic advances were made in the physical and mental health of the population.

While progress was made, it was not as rapid or extensive as many had hoped for. Others felt that the growth of social welfare policies were costing too much and posed a serious threat to the work ethic and other values inherent in individualism. In addition, the Vietnam War, inflation, and the needs of the military started to divert many resources to other areas. The New Federalism of Richard Nixon and Ronald Reagan has meant a dramatic shift away from the earlier collectivist philosophy and has involved an extensive attack on the welfare state which had developed since Franklin Roosevelt.

The New Federalism is an effort to return to a simpler and what is perceived incorrectly as a more idyllic period when the country was young and expanding westward. But the twentieth century is different from the nineteenth century, and there are limits to which social policy can be both curtailed and operated by the states and localities. Experience with the New Federalism inevitably will lead to a new approach to intergovernmental relationships which will have important consequences for social policy.

NOTES

1. *City of Clinton vs. Cedar Rapids and Missouri River Railroad Company.* 24 Iowa 455 (1868).

2. Roscoe C. Martin, *The Cities and the Federal System.* New York: Atherton Press, 1965.

3. James L. Sundquist, with the collaboration of David W. Davis. *Making Federalism Work: A Study of Program Coordination at the Community Level.* Washington, D.C.: The Brookings Institution, 1969, p. 1.

4. Francis Fox Piven & Richard A. Cloward, *Regulating the Poor: The Functions of Public Welfare.* New York: Pantheon Books, 1971.

5. Subcommittee on Intergovernmental Relations, Committee on Governmental Operation, U.S. Senate, *Creative Federalism,* 89th Congress, 2nd Session, 1966, Part I, p. 268.

6. *Ibid.*, p. 269.

7. Richard Goodwin, The Shape of American Politics. *Commentary,* June 1967, *5*, 36.

8. James L. Sundquist, *Politics and Policy: The Eisenhower, Kennedy, and Johnson Years.* Washington, D.C.: The Brookings Institution, 1968.

9. Richard P. Nathan, Statement on Revenue Sharing. Senate Subcommittee on Intergovernmental Relations, June 5, 1974, p. 4.

10. Morton H. Sklar, The Impact of Revenue Sharing on Minorities and the Poor. *Harvard Civil Rights Civil Liberties Law Review,* January 1975, 103.

11. Thomas J. Anton, Patrick Larkey, Toni Linton, Joel Epstein, John Fox, Nancy Townsend, & Claudia Zawacki, *Understanding the Fiscal Impact of General Revenue Sharing.* Ann Arbor, Mich.: Institute of Public Policy Studies, 1975.

12. Sanford F. Schram, Politics, Professionalism, and the Changing Federalism. *Social Service Review,* March 1981, pp. 78–92.

13. Robert S. Magill, Who Decides Revenue Sharing Allocations? *Social Work,* July 1977, pp. 297–300.

14. Gerald R. Wheeler, The Social Welfare Consequences of General Revenue Sharing *Public Welfare,* Summer 1972, p. 5.

15. Wilbur Cohen, The New Federalism: Theory, Practice, Problems. *National Journal,* March 1973, special report, p. 14.

Chapter 10

AMERICAN FEDERALISM AND SOCIAL POLICY

From 13 colonies, the United States grew into a large, differentiated, specialized, urbanized, and interdependent country. Industrialization, mass communications, the breakup of small communities based on mutual aid, and rising expectations have increased the need for government intervention through social policy on the regional and national level. No longer can local communities and the private sector be solely and totally responsible for problems such as poverty, old age, and mental illness. National direction becomes essential. However, as nationwide needs have been recognized and nationwide financing has become established, power has been centralized in Washington.

Over time, a reaction to such federal control has emerged. Beginning with the Creative Federalism of John Kennedy and Lyndon Johnson and strengthened by the New Federalism of Richard Nixon, Gerald Ford, and Ronald Reagan, a trend toward decreasing federal control has developed and strengthened.

In determining the relationship between the federal government and the states and localities, the founding fathers had three broad alternatives. At one extreme was the unitary form of government, with all power concentrated at the national level. At the other extreme was the model of confederation, with a weak national government and strong states. The model agreed on for America is federalism. It lies between the extremes of the unitary form and confederation.

Although American federalism lies between the two extremes, at different times in American history, it has tended toward one direction or the other. There have been four major periods of American federalism. They are distinguished partly by the relative distribution of power they confer upon the various levels of government. They also have had different consequences for social welfare policy.

Under Early Federalism, the states and the federal government were seen as equal partners. Supreme Court decisions interpreted the U.S. Constitution narrowly. All powers that were not identified specifically as federal powers reverted to the states. In general, it was felt that the least government was the best government. Social welfare services were provided mainly by local and state government and private charities.

The conditional grant-in-aid was developed during Early Federalism. It was a way for the federal government to induce the states to undertake programs that were considered in the national interest. Although developed during Early Federalism, the conditional grant-in-aid was not used extensively until the next period, Cooperative Federalism. It still is used today. Because it gives the federal government control over both goals and means, the conditional grant-in-aid is the funding device that has the most potential to centralize power at the federal level.

Cooperative Federalism emerged as the country grew in size and complexity and as problems became national in scope. The Civil War confirmed that states did not have unlimited power. The Great Depression created a national crisis that provided the opportunity for a federal response. In contrast to Early Federalism, Cooperative Federalism involved more intermingling of federal and state governmental functions. The two units of government worked together, sharing power and functions.

If Early Federalism is analogous to a two-layer cake, with one layer representing the national government and the other layer representing the state government, Cooperative Federalism is analogous to a marble cake with a mixing up of the two levels of government. During Cooperative Federalism, the federal government used the conditional grant-in-aid extensively. To some extent, the term Cooperative Federalism is misleading, because during this period the federal government increased its power significantly. Especially during the Great Depression and the two World Wars, the federal government seemed to be the more powerful of the two levels of government.

During Cooperative Federalism, the federal government provided extensive social welfare services. A series of Supreme Court decisions reflected changing beliefs about the role of government. The general welfare clause in the U.S. Constitution was interpreted as permitting the federal government to support broad social welfare services. The Social Security Act was passed in 1935. Since then, federal involvement in the broad area of social welfare has grown significantly and dramatically.

But the increase in federal power and the movement toward a unitary form of government bore the seeds of an opposite trend. With the large expansion of the number and types of conditional grants-in-aid came a degree of inefficiency and confusion, and centralization of power. Policy makers reacted with calls for simplification and less federal control through the strengthening of local and state governments. The Creative Federalism of John Kennedy and Lyndon Johnson can be seen as a beginning of the shift of some power and authority from the federal government to the states and the cities. For the first time in any major way, the cities were recognized as a part of the federal system, and grants were provided directly to them. Decentralization went a step further. Major efforts were made to involve citizens in the policy process. Much of the legislation of the time included provisions for resident participation. Finally, coordination of the diverse conditional grant-in-aid programs was emphasized under Creative Federalism.

A new funding mechanism, the block grant, was used to achieve these goals. The block grant is similar to the conditional grant-in-aid in all but one respect. Under the block grant, states and localities have the freedom to determine the means, or particular programs, that will be used to implement federal goals. The block grant thus gives more power and decision making authority to the states and localities than the conditional grant-in-aid.

The period of Creative Federalism saw an important increase in federal social welfare legislation. In a series of acts, reminiscent of the early days of Franklin D. Roosevelt, Congress passed laws in areas such as civil rights, training and employment, physical and mental health, and poverty.

The New Federalism can be seen as a continuation of the decentralization trend started under Creative Federalism. It is also a deliberate effort to eliminate some of the social welfare programs of the 1930s and 1960s.

An early feature of the New Federalism was a program called General Revenue Sharing. General Revenue Sharing sent federally collected monies back to the states, counties, and municipalities with almost no federal control. General Revenue Sharing was a radically different type of funding mechanism. Table 7 compares the powers of the different federal funding mechanisms.

Table 7: Power of Different Levels of Government and Type of Federal Grant

Conditional Grant-in-Aid	Block grant	General Revenue Sharing
High federal power	Medium federal power	Low federal power
Low state and local power	Medium state and local power	High state and local power

Table 8 combines the comparisons of the different types of federalism and the different types of federal grants.

Today, all types of federal programs are available to states and localities. All governmental units automatically receive General Revenue Sharing funds. All have the option to participate in various types of block grants and conditional grants-in-aid.

Table 8 Type of Federalism and Type of Federal Grant

Type of federalism	Type of Federal Grant		
Early Federalism (1785 to 1935)	Conditional Grant-in-aid (Federal Government specifies goals; means; states and localities apply for grant)		
Cooperative Federalism (1935 to 1960)			
Creative Federalism (1960 to 1974)		Block Grant (Federal Government specifies goals, states and localities specify means; states, localities apply for grants)	
New Federalism (1974 to present)			General Revenue Sharing (states, localities, specify goals, means; federal money automatically distributed to states and localities)

Since they have developed over the longest period of time, grant-in-aid programs are most numerous. However, the current trend is to consolidate many of the grant-in-aid programs into block grants, thus achieving some federal purpose and some state and local control.

The trend toward the block grant and away from the conditional grant-in-aid is a trend toward more state and local control and less federal control. This trend toward state and local control will diminish the resources available for social policy and hurt social welfare recipients. If the past is any guide to the future, the problems created by decentralization in the area of social welfare will lead eventually to the return to a greater federal role in social welfare policy. In the interim, however, more social policy will be made on the state and local level. It will be important for those concerned with improving social policy to understand and influence decision making on these levels.

Chapter 11

COMMUNITY DECISION MAKING

INTRODUCTION

The New Federalism focuses on local community decision making. To the extent that federal power is diminished, it is important to understand how policy decisions are made on the community level. What are the community variables that explain local decision making? Who are the most important actors? This chapter will answer these questions and other related ones.[1,2]

Reinhold Niebuhr has written that "conflict is inevitable, and in this conflict power must be challenged by power . . . The relations between groups must therefore always be predominately political rather than ethical, that is, they will be determined by the proportion of power which each group possesses at least as much as by any rational and moral appraisal for the comparative claims of each group."[3] In the past, social welfare workers often have felt that they would prevail because their cause was just and made rational sense. Rationality and a sense of justice are not enough. Power, and its exercise in the community decision making process must be understood in order to determine how social policy is made on the local level and then to be able to influence the process and the outcome.

BACKGROUND: PLURALISM AND POWER ELITES

The first major study of American communities was of Middletown (Muncie, Indiana). It was conducted by Robert and Helen Lynd in the middle 1920s and repeated in the middle 1930s. Among other aspects, their studies described a stratified social structure. The Lynds identified a small group of businessmen, who were related but not limited to a specific family. They controlled the city and their influence permeated all sectors of the community. Further individual case studies included William Lloyd Warner's description of Yankee City (Newburyport, Massachusetts) in the 1940s and August B. Hollingshead's study of Elmstown's Youth (Morris, Illinois). These early case studies, although they had varying purposes, tended to identify a stratified social system with a relatively small proportion of the population controlling major community decisions.[4]

The study of community decision making entered a modern phase with the 1953 publication of Floyd Hunter's book, *Community Power Structure*.[5] Hunter asked informants in Atlanta, Georgia to identify powerful individuals. On the basis of these interviews, Hunter concluded that a small number of businessmen and professionals constituted a power elite. He described a pyramidal power structure, in which very few individuals possessed the potential to affect community decision making.

John Walton writes that *Community Power Structure* can be called a classic. Its lasting significance stems partly from Hunter's creation of the term "power structure." This term has been used extensively by social scientists and political activists. Hunter also formulated a new method for studying community power structures. This method has come to be called the reputational approach. Since *Community Power Structure* was published, more than 500 books and articles have been written on the topic.[6]

After the publication of Hunter's work, case studies of other cities were undertaken. They often used different methods and studied different communities. They generally did not find as centralized a power structure as Hunter did.

The most famous of the studies that seemed to contradict Hunter were Robert A. Dahl's *Who Governs?* and Edward C. Banfield's *Political Influence.*[7] Dahl studied decisions in New Haven, Connecticut, and Banfield studied decision making in Chicago, Illinois. Using a method different from Hunter's, they reconstructed specific decisions in a few community issue areas.

Both Dahl and Banfield looked at major community controversies. In reconstructing each community conflict, efforts were made to determine how the controversy was started, who were the opposing actors, who mediated the conflict, how the conflict was resolved, and who benefited from the resolution. Hunter's centralized power structure model would have been confirmed if in different community decisions, in different policy areas, the same individuals and groups became involved and were able to control the outcomes. However, Banfield and Dahl and other researchers found that group and institutional involvement was determined by the issue. Educational issues involved one set of participants. Social welfare controversies involved different individuals and groups. Community conflicts relating to business issues involved still other participants. In Norton Long's phrase, the local community was "an ecology of games."[8] Each actor attempted to maximize his or her advantage in terms of his or her self-interest and became active only if the decision directly affected him or her. Some actors, primarily the mayor, were involved across many issue areas.

While pluralists admitted that not all members were equally involved in decision making, they rejected the idea of a single power elite ruling community life for their own best interests. The pluralists felt that there was relatively wide sharing of power among different leaders who specialize in one or a few issue areas. Further, there were constraints which were placed upon both elites and nonelites, and conditions created by outside forces that affected decision making.[9]

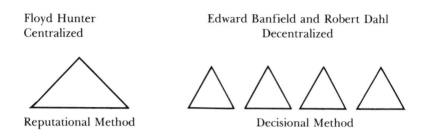

Floyd Hunter   Edward Banfield and Robert Dahl
Centralized   Decentralized

Reputational Method   Decisional Method

Figure 3: Different Power Structures

Figure 3 shows the different community power structures of Floyd Hunter and of Edward Banfield and Robert Dahl.

The differences between the elitists, the followers of Hunter, and the pluralists, the followers of Dahl and Banfield, produced intense debate. Dahl and the pluralists criticized Hunter's method. They suggested that by creating a relatively small panel and asking panel members to identify a few community leaders who had the reputation for being powerful, there was a greater probability of identifying a small power structure. Further, the pluralists said Hunter was not studying the exercise of power or influence, but just the potential to use power. To discover who really governs, one must make case studies of individual decisions.[10]

The elitists also criticized the pluralists. For example, William Domhoff restudied New Haven and attempted to refute Dahl's analysis point by point. He concluded that New Haven was ruled by a small elite who also were part of a national elite. In Domhoff's words, "Our work at the national level and the present findings on New Haven support the idea that there remains a priviledged class in America which also provides the economic leadership of society."[11]

The approaches of the elitists and the pluralists defined alternative conceptions of community power. Followers of Hunter and of Dahl and Banfield sought to extend the initial results by conducting additional case studies of decision making in individual cities. By the mid-1960s, studies of 166 cities had been completed. Efforts to compare them quantitatively, however, suggested the unreliability, or at least the low comparability, of the different case studies.[12]

In the late 1960s comparative studies of two, three, or four communities were undertaken, and a shift in perspective began to emerge.[13] A general continuum ranging from centralization to decentralization was recognized as more accurate empirically than the conceptions of either elitism or pluralism. Socioeconomic characteristics of communities were linked with centralization in a series of propositions amenable to empirical testing.

Also generally recognized was the conceptual distinction between power as the access to resources and influence as the making of concrete decisions. Thus, power refers to potential, but not necessarily to exercized influence. Influence is conceived of as the making of decisions that cause change. Correspondingly, a power structure (a patterned distribution of power) could be distinguished from a decision making structure (a patterned distribution of influence).[14] The reputational approach of Hunter was thus seen as operationalizing power, while the decisional approach of Dahl and Banfield was an operationalization of influence. Results from the two methods should not have been expected to be identical, since two different phenomena were being studied. This conceptual distinction clarified earlier conflicting results.

There are several general points of agreement among the major studies of community decision making. There is a general consensus, for example, that power and influence are distributed differentially in a community among leaders, participants, and the general population. Only a small percentage of a community's citizens actively participate in community decision making. The distribution of power and influence does have an effect on what gets done, what does not get done, and who benefits. Although the power structure and decision making structure variables are not the only or always the most significant variables that determine what gets done and who benefits, they must be considered in any study of community decision making.

A second point of general agreement is that through a variety of techniques, leadership structures can be identified reliably and validly. Generally, leaders comprise a small percentage of the total population and often are aligned with or selected from top political and business sectors. Other interests also may be represented.

A third point is that the organizational structures of a city are important in explaining power arrangements and policy outcomes. Public agencies, corporations, voluntary associations and ethnic, neighborhood, and civil rights organizations all can affect the community decision making process, either individually or in coalitions. Democratic participation, such as voting and direct action by interest groups, also can have an effect on policy.[15]

A MODEL OF COMMUNITY DECISION MAKING

These conclusions are all very broad. In addition to these general areas of agreement, studies of community decision making have identified a series of variables that could be important in describing and affecting the community decision making process. The old distinction between elitists and pluralists has been seen as too simplistic. Additional factors contribute to the community decision making process.

Fundamental variables important in community decision making are summarized in an input-throughput-output flow chart, shown in Figure 4.[16] Similar figures appear in several studies.

"Inputs to the community" and "national societal characteristics" act as general constraints on local decision making, mediated by "community characteristics" (demographic, economic, legal-political, organizational, cultural). These variables, in turn, influence "centralization of power and decision making" and "leadership." Leadership is defined in terms of the characteristics of leaders (e.g., businesspeople versus politicians). In turn, these variables generate "policy outputs," such as expenditures for social services. Finally, policy outputs feed back on earlier variables to exert "policy impacts," or changes resulting from the policy outputs such as decreased social problems.

Several large scale comparative studies were undertaken in

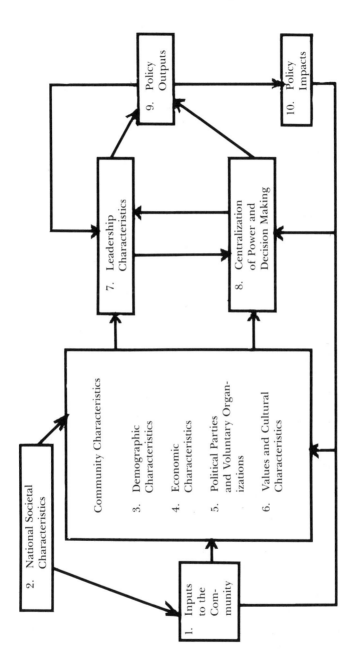

Figure 4: Fundamental Variables in Community Decision Making

an effort to estimate precise empirical relationships among variables of the sort depicted in Figure 4. Perhaps the most ambitious efforts in establishing the relationships among variables occurred in the Permanent Community Sample of the National Opinion Research Center at the University of Chicago. The study was of 51 communities, with populations ranging from 50,000 to 750,000.[17]

RESEARCH METHODS FOR STUDYING COMMUNITY POWER AND INFLUENCE

Three basic methods have been used for measuring power and influence: the positional method, the reputational method, and the decisional method. The positional approach was developed by C. Wright Mills, soon after Hunter's study. Mills felt that America was ruled by a power elite who gained their power because of their economic position in society.[18] The positional method begins by establishing a list of occupants of important positions in the community, such as the mayor, the head of the largest business, and the editor of the major newspaper. Generally, some kind of information then is collected about these leaders, such as social background data from published sources. Problems with this approach include difficulty in developing valid criteria for the selection of important positions and then in inferring the amount of influence wielded.

For the reputational approach, first used by Floyd Hunter, a panel of community informants is created. The panel is asked to identify leaders as defined by a particular criterion. For example, the panel might be asked to identify "persons who are important in getting things done in this town." Results then may be summarized, as in the positional method. A disadvantage of the reputational method is that it tends to assume a pyramidal structure, at least in the sense that it does not distinguish explicitly separate issue areas or levels of involvement in decisions. The reputational approach also is based on the knowledge of the panel of community informants. An uninformed panel will result in inaccurate conclusions.

A variation of this approach is the issue-specific reputational approach, in which informants are asked to rank or score individual community actors in terms of their power in specific issue areas. As in the 51 Community Study, informants may be asked, "If someone wanted to initiate a social welfare program in this community, how important would the support of the following actors be?" The informant then scores a list of actors on a scale from high to low.

The method thus does not assume generality of power, but makes possible the empirical analysis of leadership across issue areas. Both the reputational method and the issue-specific reputational method are used to operationalize power instead of influence, because of their focus on potential rather than on exercised influence.

Finally, there is the decisional method used initially by Dahl and by Banfield. The decisional method involves tracing the history of a specific decision or decisions through its basic stages. For example, the investigator studies who initiated an action, who supported this action, who opposed it, who mediated between the conflicting groups, and who prevailed. By studying several community decisions, it is possible to determine whether a few actors are influential in all areas or if many different actors participate in the decision making structure.

The decisional method helps to identify leaders according to their degree of involvement. But the approach does not identify indirect influence. Further, in reconstructing a community controversy, it is usually difficult to get all of the information. Therefore, supporters of Hunter charged that cities may be centralized, with a few leaders controlling important decisions. The identities of these actors are kept secret from the investigator using the decisional method. Further, the decisional method relies heavily on the objectivity of the investigator. An investigator looking for a decentralized structure may overlook contrary indications. Also, it is often impractical to study each community decision as carefully as this approach requires.

According to Domhoff, the three approaches can be used simultaneously. Names of powerful people can be generated by all of the methods. The task of the researcher is then to describe the relations among important actors, including kinship ties, social connections, and interlocking directorates. In addition, there should be an analysis of the flow of money into and out of the power network and a content analysis of important communications, such as speeches, books, and memoranda. "Power structure research involves mapping networks of people, institutions, and money flows, and then doing content analysis of the verbal and written outputs of these networks."[19]

Community Variables

Community variables shown in Figure 4, *Fundamental Variables in Community Decision Making,* are described in detail below.

Inputs to the Community

Extralocal policies and programs all affect the community. Their different forms, conditional grant-in-aid, block grant, General Revenue Sharing, or court decisions, affect the degree of community autonomy differently. Roland Warren wrote in *The Community in America*[20] that communities have faced the loss of their autonomy and a lack of identification of residents with the community. These changes result primarily from the increase and type of community inputs. Warren believes that the old horizontal pattern of relationships among community institutions has been replaced somewhat by vertical relationships between community institutions and extralocal community units, such as the federal government. This change weakens the community as an integrated social system. Warren recommended a community development strategy aimed at restoring the cohesion of the community.[21] The loss of power and control by the local community has been criticized by supporters of the New Federalism, who are working to increase the power of community decision making.

Community Characteristics

Community characteristics traditionally have been used to explain variations in community decision making. Generally speaking, the more varied the demographic, economic, and political base of the community, the more the community will be decentralized. Conversely, homogenity of community characteristics is associated with centralized decision making structures.

Size of community is one index of complexity. Smaller communities tend to be more homogeneous, while larger communities tend to be more diverse. The existing research shows that smaller communities are more centralized than larger communities.[22]

In addition to size, the ethnic characteristics of a community affect the degree of decentralization. Generally speaking, communities that have a few different ethnic groups tend to be more centralized than are communities which have many different ethnic groups.

More recently, it has been found that the size of the middle and lower class sectors in a community can have an important effect on policy output. Generally speaking, during the 1960s communities which had larger lower income populations tended to spend more on policies directed toward their benefit. Conversely, communities with larger middle class populations tended to be more concerned with lower property taxes.[23] Communities which have large percentages of retired persons, in Florida and in the Southwest, have emphasized policies for older Americans.

The number and size of industries affect the degree of centralization. Communities dominated by one large employer whose headquarters are located in the area are almost always centralized. On the other hand, decentralization is associated with a diversified economic base.

Political parties and voluntary organizations are important in community decision making. Centralized communities tend to have only one major party or a system of nonpartisan elections. Voluntary associations tend to be small, few in number, and inactive. In contrast, many active voluntary organizations, at least two political parties, and partisan elections are associated with more decentralized decision making systems.

Political scientists have been interested in the consequences of the structure of city government on policy outputs. When policy outputs are considered, how do cities with a strong mayor differ from those with a council-manager type of government? In the 51 Communities, those with council-manager governments tend to spend more, in general, than those with a strong mayor. The structure of government, therefore, must be considered in any study of community decision making.

The extent to which opinions and values influence policy is a topic of current concern. Verba and Nie have shown that upper class persons, who participate and are effective to a greater degree than middle and lower class persons, are also more conservative than the population in general. Verba and Nie conclude that because of this fact, social policy at all levels of government is more sensitive to upper class interests and more conservative than the general population.[24]

A recent approach to community decision making suggests that the most important determinants of policy are the beliefs and preferences of the majority of the citizens. This theory has been called populist theory. Populist theory suggests that elected politicians strive to become responsive to the voters in general and hesitate to make decisions which they feel will be unpopular.[25]

Leadership

A central concern in urban areas is who exerts power and influence. The earliest case studies showed businesspeople to be most central. At other times, the mayor and political actors were seen as most important. Some studies showed businesspeople and politicians collaborating in differing degrees with other community actors. Not surprisingly, the comparative studies revealed similar diversity. But the diversity of the comparative studies is nevertheless structured. There are consistent results that have recurred in enough cities to make them notable.

Recent studies identify two patterns of city leadership: one centered around the mayor and his or her office and a second centered on business leaders, and newspapers.[26] The relative mixture, however, varies considerably across cities. Although there are a few cities where the mayor and his or her office are central actors, and others where business actors are more central, most cities have diverse coalitions involving these and other actors in varying mixes. Nevertheless, in most cities the three key actors remain the mayor, leading businesspeople, and the newspaper editor and/or publisher.

The comparative studies distinguish two general tendencies that differentiate cities. One tendency includes patterns more associated with business and newspaper leadership. Elite civic groups and the chamber of commerce also are likely to be important actors in these business-oriented cities. Business-oriented cities tend to be found more often in the Western United States, in cities that have smaller populations, city managers, nonpartisan at large elections, and more affluent citizens who tend to vote Republican. By contrast, political actors, especially the mayor, political parties, and sometimes labor union leaders and heads of government agencies tend to be more important in the Midwest and the Eastern United States and in cities with larger populations, more industry, mayor-council government, partisan and ward based elections, middle income residents, Roman Catholics, and immigrants from central and southern Europe. In most instances, however, such generalizations are clearer and more consistent for the power structure than for the decision making structure.[27]

Centralization

Centralization often is conceptualized and measured in two dimensions: participation and overlap. The larger the number of participants and the less their overlap across issue areas, the less centralized the community's power structure or decision making structure.

As previously noted, communities are likely to have more decentralized power and decision making structures if they

> are large in population,
>
> have a diversified ethnic population,
>
> are diversified economically (many employers and many types of employers),

have more than one political party, and
have active voluntary associations.

The extent of decentralization has practical implications for influencing social policy. In more decentralized structures, it is important to form coalitions of institutions. For example, an effort to increase programs for children in decentralized communities might attempt to enlist support from business, labor, mass communications, religion, and education as well as from social welfare workers. In a more centralized community, efforts to influence community social policy should be directed towards the most influential persons in the decision making structure.

Policy Outputs

Policy outputs are the result of collective and mainly governmental decision making. They traditionally have been measured by fiscal indicators,[28] such as the amount of money that a community spends on social services.

At least two factors may be important when considering the policy output of more centralized and more decentralized decision making structures. The first factor is whether the policy is a more public or a more separable good. The second is the degree to which a policy is controversial.

A pure public good is produced by government and consumed by all citizens. A public good may be supplied jointly to several individuals without the increased use of one individual affecting the availability of the good for other individuals. An example is fluoridation. If individual A consumes fluoridated water, so does individual B. A's use level does not decrease B's. In contrast, separable goods may benefit one group in the population while taking resources from others. Providing social services for one group in a city results in fewer resources available for other groups in a city.

Controversial decisions deal with policies and programs that are new to a community and with relatively unpopular policies and programs that benefit less powerful members of the community.[29]

Conceptually, continua can be developed for public goods and controversial decisions. Every policy output can be located somewhere on each continuum. Many programs of interest to social workers that benefit distinct sections of the population, such as the poor and emotionally ill, tend to be separable. Community decisions around social policy are therefore harder to implement and require knowledge and skill in community decision making.

RECENT RESEARCH ON COMMUNITY DECISION MAKING

Recent studies have tended to support the general model of community decision making presented earlier, although different studies have emphasized different aspects. In addition, there have been important qualifications which have limited somewhat the applicability of the model. Bachrach and Baratz point out that the community decision making research has not taken nondecisions into account. Often these nondecisions are as important as decisions, although the process of decision making may be different from the process used in ordinary decision making.[30] This process has been called the "second face of power." Polsby believes that the failure to consider nondecisions is a problem that presents empirical difficulties, some of which can be overcome, but it does not invalidate the major findings of the community decision making studies. He notes that the "findings about the second face of power do not erase findings about the first face."[31]

In an important contribution, Larry Lyon and Charles Bonjean suggest that policies differ in the degree to which they are routine. Routine policies are those which are not related to the distribution of community power. Routine policies tend to be made by administrators, are of an incremental nature, are noncontroversial, and do not involve the whole panoply of community decision making. Less routine decisions do involve changes in the distribution of power and often are associated with community controversy. They affect a larger number of citizens, including the top leadership of the community. According to Lyon and Bonjean, many community decisions are routine and do not involve the top leadership of a community.[32]

A related study, which asserts that business elites are concerned primarily with growth, from which they benefit, concludes that ". . . if an output is not an important concern of the elite, there is no necessary relationship between power and policy."[33]

Terry Clark and Lorna Ferguson have shown that different factors in the community decision making model are significant at different times in the history of a community. In studying urban fiscal policy, Clark and Ferguson determined that citizen preferences, organized groups, and political leaders were most important in determining community policies during the past 20 years. During the 1960s, cities with large Black populations and active interest groups increased their expenditures. The increase was less in cities with large middle class populations. The early 1970s was a period of greater political instability. Organized groups were not as powerful, and political leadership had more flexibility. During this period, city budgets increased in cities where riots had occurred and where large ethnic and religious groups supported the mayor in his election. City budgets did not increase as much where the mayor exerted leadership in the area of economy in government efforts. Finally, during the later part of the '70s, citizens in all communities became more fiscally conservative. Their strong preferences were for lower taxes, and cities were forced to reduce their spending.[34]

In general, earlier studies of community decision making were concerned with the question of who governs. This question still is seen as important. Yet more recent studies have tended to study who benefits from community decision making and the identification of factors in community decision making which can be associated with certain types of policies. With the increasing decentralization of social policy from the federal to the state and community level, this effort is important and should continue in social welfare.

COMMUNITY DECISION MAKING FOR SOCIAL WELFARE

A recent study was made of factors which contribute to support for social welfare allocations on the community level under different types of American Federalism.[35] The study concluded that social welfare policy decisions tended to be separable and controversial. In other words, there is little support for social welfare on the community level. When social welfare programs for those in need or on the local level are considered, there must be some nonlocal controls directing municipalities to spend money for social welfare clients.

When the types of variables important in explaining grants for social welfare at the local level are considered, political and voluntary associational activity measures occur most often. Cities which were relatively generous in the allocation of General Revenue Sharing monies for those in need were also cities in which there appeared to be strong and active voluntary associations which were exerting pressure on officials for these monies. Surprisingly, allocations for social services under General Revenue Sharing were inversely related to measures of need, such as unemployment. Cities with high rates of unemployment tended to allocate less money for social welfare than did cities with low rates of unemployment, when there was local control.[36]

SUMMARY

This chapter has reviewed the historical, conceptual, and empirical development of the study of community decision making. Based on past research, the variables of input to the community, demographic characteristics, economic characteristics, structure of local government, political parties, and voluntary organizations, values and cultural characteristics, leadership characteristics, and centralization all are seen to contribute to policy outputs at the local level.

When the federal government plans for less federal involvement in social policy, more social policy decisions will be made on the state and local level of government. Therefore, knowledge of community decision making and ways of influencing it will be crucial to those concerned with social policy.

NOTES

1. This chapter is based on Robert S. Magill & Terry N. Clark, Community Power and Decision Making; Recent Research and its Policy Implications. *Social Service Review*, March 1975, *49*, 33–45; Robert S. Magill, Who Decides Revenue Sharing Allocations? *Social Work*, July 1977, pp. 297–300; Robert S. Magill. *Community Decision Making for Social Welfare: Federalism, City Government and the Poor.* New York: Human Sciences Press, 1979.

2. Many terms are used in a specific way in this chapter. Unless otherwise stated, "community" refers to a legal-geographical entity, such as a city or a suburb, which is the arena for decision making about public policy. "Community Variables" include all the independent variables that could explain policy on the community level.

3. Reinhold Niebuhr, *Moral Man and Immoral Society: A Study In Ethics and Politics.* New York: Charles Scribner, 1960.

4. Cited in Nelson W. Polsby, *Community Power and Political Theory: A Further Look at Problems of Evidence and Inference,* (2nd, enlarged ed.). New Haven: Yale University Press, 1980.

5. Floyd Hunter, *Community Power Structure: A Study of Decision Makers.* Chapel Hill, N.C.: University of North Carolina Press, 1953.

6. John Walton, The Bearing of Social Science Research on Public Issues: Floyd Hunter and the Study of Power. In John Walton & Donald E. Carns. *Cities in Change: Studies on the Urban Social Condition,* (2nd ed.). Boston: Allyn & Bacon, 1977, pp. 263–272.

7. Edward C. Banfield, *Political Influence.* New York: The Free Press, 1960; Robert A. Dahl, *Who Governs? Democracy Power in an American City.* New Haven: Yale University Press, 1961.

8. Norton Long, The Local Community as an Ecology of Games. *American Journal of Sociology,* 1958, *64*, pp. 251–61.

9. Polsby. *ibid.*

10. Walton, *ibid.*

11. G. William Domhoff, *Who Really Rules? New Haven and Community Power Reexamined.* New Brunswick: Transaction Books, 1978, p. 32.

12. Terry N. Clark, *Community Power and Policy Outputs: A Review of Urban Research.* Beverly Hills, California: Sage Publications, 1973.

13. Robert Agger, Daniel Goldrich, & Bert Swanson, *The Rulers and the Ruled: Political Power and Impotence in American Communities.* New York: John Wiley, 1964; Michael Aiken & Paul Mott, (eds.). *The Structure of Community Power.* New York: Random House, 1970; Terry N. Clark, *Community Structure and Decision-Making: Comparative Analyses.* Scranton, Penn.: Chandler Publishing, 1968; Robert Presthus, *Men at the Top: A Study of Community Power.* New York: Oxford University Press, 1964.

14. Clark, *Community Structure and Decision-Making,* pp. 46–47.

15. Walton, *ibid.*

16. Robert T. Crain, Elihu Katz, & Donald B. Rosenthal, *The Politics of Community Conflict: The Fluoridation Decision.* Indianapolis: Bobbs-Merrill, 1967; Brian T. Downes, (ed.). *Cities and Suburbs: Selected Readings in Local Politics and Public Policy.* Belmont, California: Wadsworth Publishing, 1971.

17. Terry N. Clark, Community Structure, Decision-Making, Budget Expenditures, and Urban Renewal in 51 American Communities. *American Sociological Review,* August 1968, *33,* pp. 576–593.

18. David Ricci, Receiving Ideas in Political Analysis: The Case of Community Power Studies 1950–1970. *The Western Political Quarterly,* December 1980, *33:4,* pp. 451–475.

19. Domhoff, *ibid,* p. 145.

20. Roland Warren, *The Community in America* (2nd ed.). Chicago: Rand McNally, 1972.

21. *Ibid.*

22. Michael Aiken & Robert Atford, Community Structure and Innovation. In T.N. Clark, (ed.), *Comparative Community Politics,* 1974.

23. Terry N. Clark & Lorna C. Ferguson, *City Money.* New York: Columbia University Press, 1983.

24. Sidney Verba & Norman H. Nie, *Participation in America.* New York: Harper & Row, 1972.

25. Paul D. Schumaker, Russell W. Getter, Terry N. Clark, *Policy Responsiveness and Fiscal Strain in 51 American Communities.* Washington, D.C.: The American Political Science Association, 1979, pp. 20–21.

26. Terry N. Clark, Leadership in American Cities: Resources, Interchanges and the Press. Unpublished manuscript, Chicago, June 1973; Edward O. Laumann, Lois M. Verbrugge, & Franz U. Pappi, A Causal Modeling Approach to the Study of a Community Elite's Influence Structure. *American Sociological Review,* April 1974, *39,* 16–174; Laura A. Morlock. Business Interests, Countervailing Groups and the Balance of Influence in 91 Cities. In *The Search for Community Power,* (2nd ed.). Willard D. Hawley & Frederick M. Wirt (eds.). Englewood Cliffs, NJ: Prentice Hall, 1974; Peter H. Rossi, Richard A. Berk & Bettye K. Eidson. *The Roots of Urban Discontent.* New York: Wiley Interscience, 1974. Anne S. Williams, Relationships Between the Structure of Local Influence and Policy Outcomes. *Rural Sociology,* 1980, *45*(4), 621–643.

27. Clark, T.N., "Leadership in American Cities.

28. Clark, T.N., *Community Power and Policy Outputs,* p. 63.

29. *Ibid.*

30. P. Backrach & M.S. Baratz, The Two Faces of Power. *American Political Science Review,* 1962, *56,* pp. 947–52.

31. Nelson W. Polsby, Empirical Investigation of the Mobilization of Bias in Community Power Research, *Political Studies,* December 1979, *27:4,* 541.

32. Larry Lyon, & Charles M. Bonjean, Community Power and Policy Outputs: The Routines of Local Politics. *Urban Affairs Quarterly,* September 1981, *17:1,*3–21.

33. Larry Lyon, Lawrence G., Felice, M. Ray Perryman, & S. Parker, Community Power and Population Increase: An Empirical Test of

the Growth Machine Model. *American Journal of Sociology,* May 1981, *86:6,* p. 1397.

34. Clark and Ferguson, *ibid.*
35. Robert S. Magill, *Community Decision Making for Social Welfare.*
36. *Ibid.*

Part IV

A MODEL FOR THE DEVELOPMENT AND ANALYSIS OF SOCIAL POLICY

Chapter 12

AN INTRODUCTION TO POLICY
ANALYSIS AND DEVELOPMENT

INTRODUCTION

Models for developing social policy proliferated during the 1960s, when there was strong public and private support for social welfare. Alfred Kahn,[1] Franklin Zweig and Robert Morris,[2] Robert Perlman and Arnold Gurin,[3] Howard Freeman and Clarence Sherwood,[4] and others created approaches designed to guide those concerned with creating new social policies and social programs.

As resources available for social policy have become more limited and as questions are raised about existing policies, efforts have increased to develop models to analyze current social policies. Neil Gilbert and Harry Specht,[5] David Gil,[6] Charles Prigmore and Charles R. Atherton,[7] Theodore Marmor,[8] Thomas R. Dye,[9] and others have described approaches for the analysis of existing social policy.

Traditionally, policy analysis, in contrast to policy development, has concentrated on studying existing policies. Policy analysts, according to scholars, should refrain from making pro-

167

posals for the future. This responsibility belongs to policy developers.

For example, Martin Rein has defined policy analysis as accounting for the development of policy by explaining the choices and assumptions which were made as the policy was developed. The policy analyst, for Rein, does not make suggestions about how the policy can be improved. Policy development, on the other hand, involves converting value choices into programs. This conversion occurs when developers choose among alternatives in order to reach a goal which has been agreed upon.[10] Similarly, Thomas Dye[11] feels that policy analysis is concerned primarily with explanation rather than prescription. Policy analysis involves a careful investigation into the causes and consequences of policies. Policy analysis does not include making proposals.[12]

Yet both policy analysis and policy development should focus on the content and consequences of social policy. Analysis looks at policies already in effect; development provides guidelines for creating new policies. Therefore, it is logical and useful to create a model which can be used for both policy analysis and policy development. The remainder of this chapter and the next chapters will describe a model which can be used for both policy analysis and policy development. For the sake of convenience, the model will be described in the present tense.

A POLICY ANALYSIS–POLICY DEVELOPMENT MODEL

A policy analysis–policy development model flows from the earlier definition of social policy. Social policy has been defined as general principles and courses of action developed to achieve social goals. Since there often is conflict among competing goals and also among competing means, policy analysis and policy development involve understanding and making choices between alternatives. These choices are resolved by research and rational thought, value orientations, and political considerations. Therefore, a policy analysis model which will be able to account for choices already made must analyze these choices in terms of the effects of research and rationality, of underlying values, and of relevant political considerations. For a model to be helpful in guiding the policy development process, it must consider choices based on the same elements—research and rationality, values, and politics.

The areas of research and rationality, values, and politics potentially are important at each stage of the policy process. Of course, it is possible that some policies will be developed almost totally in terms of one factor or of a combination of only some of these factors. For example, political factors often are more important than research and rationality.

Research and rationality refer to different but related aspects. Research refers to knowledge, gained through observation and experiment, which helps in making policy choices. To look at a policy choice from a research point of view requires asking if there is any evidence to support one policy approach over another. Rationality refers to logic and internal consistency. Are various parts of a policy interrelated to make rational sense together? Is the policy logical and internally consistent?

Policies can be made and analyzed in terms of values, opinions, and beliefs. While scholars have made distinctions between them, for this model, beliefs, opinions, and values will be combined and referred to as values. Simply, values are conceptions of what is desirable. Values can be seen also as criteria for making a decision about what is desirable. Values usually are stated in general terms, at a high level of abstraction.[13] For example, typical American values include democracy, equality, individual freedom, social mobility, responsibility, and working rather than "taking charity." These values and others can be very important in determining social welfare policy.

Politics, for our purposes, is concerned with the way policies are developed and changed in a democracy. More specifically, politics refers to the individuals and organized interest groups which participate in and try to influence the process of policy development.

A social policy has several aspects. These aspects include a statement of the social problem and a statement of the way in which the policy is going to be implemented. Finally, there should be some consideration of the consequences of the policy.

Choices are made in determining each of these aspects.

Therefore, in simplified form, the policy analysis–policy development model is:

Table 9: Policy Analysis–Policy Development Model

	RESEARCH & RATIONALITY	VALUES	POLITICS
Definition of the Social Problem			
Implementation of the Social Policy			
Consequences of the Social Policy			

SPECIAL CONSIDERATIONS IN USING THE POLICY ANALYSIS–POLICY DEVELOPMENT MODEL

The range of social policies is very broad. This model was developed to be applicable to all social policies. Parts of the model might not be relevant to a specific policy and should be ignored. Other parts of the model, while important, might be impractical to use. For example, in policy analysis politics are extremely important for understanding why specific choices were made. However, it is often difficult to discover, unless one was a participant in the process, many of the deals and compromises which individuals and interest groups made. Similarly, while the policy developer should consider the political aspects of a proposal, it is often difficult to predict with precision the constellation of individuals and groups, their skill and their power, and their support and opposition to various aspects of a proposed policy.

Difficulties also can be encountered under research and rationality. There is a growing recognition that the selection of a research problem is influenced by values and the interests of significant individuals and groups. Thus, from the beginning, the research enterprise may not be completely objective.[14]

Unfortunately, the data for making rational policy decisions in social welfare often are not available in a useful form or at all.

This relative unavailability is caused in part by the complexity of the phenomena social policies are concerned with. Also relevant is the difficulty of establishing relationships between a specific social welfare program and an identified outcome of individual and/or social change. The factors of time, energy, and expense tend to discourage careful program evaluation. Finally, higher priority is given usually to developing and operating programs rather than to studying them.

There are also problems inherent in linking social science research and governmental decision making. Social scientists tend to study broad problems. Governmental decision makers, however, typically have a limited range of policy options which often are not addressed by the available research. Further, governmental officials and social scientists have difficulty in predicting future research needs, so studies often are made of past problems. The results are not useful, when they are available, for present decision making.

Even when research is current and relevant, it is not always used. Government officials are generally suspicious of the validity and reliability of social policy research. Further, in a recent survey, 75 percent of government officials responded that they ignored research that did not coincide with their own beliefs.[15]

This relative lack of generally accepted scientific research makes the development of effective social policy harder. Since it is more difficult to cite established authorities to resolve policy conflicts, the roles of values and politics become more important. If research cannot suggest that a particular policy will be effective, political pressures and opinions become more important in the process of policy formulation.

The Policy Analysis–Policy Development Model does not weight or rank aspects of the model in terms of importance. For a given policy, however, political factors may be more important than rationality. Further, within specific phases of the policy, definition of the problem, implementation of the policy, and consequences of the policy, and within the aspects of the model, research and rationality, values, and politics, specific questions might be more important than others. For example, the fact that a specific policy is not rational, e.g., that the problem definition,

Table 10: A Policy Analysis-Policy Development Model

Definition of the Social Problem	*Research and Rationality*
What is the social problem?	Is the definition of the problem rational and consistent with existing research?
Who is affected directly by the problem?	Is this description of the client group at the appropriate level of generality and consistent with existing research? Are the criteria used to select clients supported by research and rationality?
How was the problem caused?	Does the existing research support the cause(s)?

Implementation of the Social Policy	
What are the goals and objectives of the policy?	Are the goals and objectives consistent with existing research and do they relate logically to the definition of the problem?
What provisions implement the policy?	What are the provisions? Does existing research support the provisions selected to implement the policy?
What is the organizational structure of the administering agency?	Is the organizational structure appropriate for the policy?
How is the policy to be financed?	Is the financing adequate, predictable, and provided in the proper form based on research and rationality?

Consequences of the Social Policy	
What are the costs and benefits of the policy?	Are the costs and benefits appropriate in terms of research and rationality?
What are the consequences of the policy for the clients, the social system, and the social service system?	What are the intended and unintended consequences of the policy in terms of research and rationality?

Values	*Politics*
Is this an important social problem?	Is this definition of the problem politically feasible?
What values are important in the selection of the client group? Are these appropriate values?	What individuals and groups, if any, support and which oppose this definition of the client group? What effect, if any, does this have on the definition of the problem?
What values are important in determining the causes(s) of the problem? Are these appropriate values?	What effect, if any, do individuals and groups have on selection of causes?
What values affect the goals and objectives? Are these values appropriate?	What are the relative levels of power of competing policies? How does this affect the policy?
Does the policy treat clients appropriately in terms of equality, equity, adequacy and client self-determination?	Is there sufficient support to give the policy a reasonable chance of being acted upon?
Will the organizational structure promote efficient and effective service delivery?	What groups and individuals benefit from this policy? Who loses? What effect does this have on implementation?
Is the financing adequate, predictable, and provided in the proper form based on values?	Is the financing adequate, predictable, and provided in the proper form based on politics?
Are the costs and benefits appropriate in terms of values?	Are the costs and benefits appropriate in terms of politics?
What are the intended and unintended consequences of the policy in terms of values?	How do support and opposition to the policy at the community level affect the delivery of services?

the goals and the means, and the client group do not relate to one another, might be less important than the political support and opposition which the policy engenders.

In conclusion, the policy analyst in looking at an existing policy might find that some aspects of the model are not at all relevant to the policy under consideration. Further, for some aspects which are relevant, it might be too difficult to obtain important material. Finally, of those aspects which are relevant and obtainable, some aspects will be more important in explaining the policy than others. The more important aspects should be given most attention. Likewise, the policy developer will want to emphasize at each stage of the process those aspects of the model which seem to be most significant as the policy unfolds.

THE COMPLETE POLICY ANALYSIS–POLICY DEVELOPMENT MODEL

Table 10 presents the complete Policy Analysis–Policy Development Model which will be described in the subsequent chapters.

NOTES

1. Alfred J. Kahn, *Theory and Practice of Social Planning.* New York: Russell Sage Foundation, 1969.

2. Franklin Zweig and Robert Morris, The Social Planning Design Guide: Process and Proposal, *Social Work,* 1966, pp. 13–21.

3. Robert Perlman and Arnold Gurin, *Community Organization and Social Planning.* New York: John Wiley & Sons, 1972.

4. Howard Freeman and Clarence Sherwood, *Social Research and Social Policy.* Englewood Cliffs, New Jersey: Prentice-Hall, 1970.

5. Neil Gilbert and Harry Specht, *Dimensions of Social Welfare Policy.* Englewood Cliffs, New Jersey: Prentice-Hall, Inc., 1974.

6. David Gil, *Unraveling Social Policy: Theory, Analysis, and Political Action Towards Social Equality.* Cambridge: Schenkman Publishing Co., 1973.

7. Charles S. Prigmore and Charles R. Atherton, *Social Welfare Policy: Analysis and Formulation.* Lexington, Massachusetts: D.C. Heath and Company, 1979.

8. Theodore Marmor, *The Politics of Medicare.* Chicago: Aldine, 1973.

9. Thomas R. Dye, *Understanding Public Policy.* Englewood Cliffs, New Jersey: Prentice-Hall, Inc., 1972.

10. Martin Rein, *Social Policy: Issues of Choice and Change.* N.Y.: Random House, 1970.

11. Dye, *ibid.*

12. Rein, *ibid.*

13. Kahn, *ibid.*

14. Michael Hibbard, The Crisis in Social Policy Planning, *Social Service Review,* December, 1981, 557–567; Martin Rein and Lisa Peattie, Knowledge for Policy, *Social Service Review,* December, 1981, pp. 525–543.

15. Donald Brieland, Use of Research-Measuring the Unmeasurable: An Essay Review, *Social Work Research and Abstracts,* Winter, 1981, pp. 40–43; a review of Carol H. Weiss with Michael Bucuvalas, *Social Science Research and Decision-Making.* N. Y.: Columbia U. Press, 1980.

Chapter 13

DEFINITION OF THE
SOCIAL PROBLEM

INTRODUCTION

This chapter will present the first phase of the model, definition of the social problem. Social problems should be defined in terms of research and rationality, values, and politics. More specifically, there are three questions which should be answered in order to define a social problem. They are:

What is the social problem?

Who is affected directly by the problem?

How was the problem caused?

WHAT IS THE SOCIAL PROBLEM?

Research and Rationality. Is the definition of the social problem rational and consistent with existing research?

The social problem should be described as completely as possible. For example, if poverty is the problem, a description could include the income level below which a family of four would be considered to be living in poverty. Other aspects of poverty, such as inadequate food, clothing, and shelter, and a general lack of ability to control one's life also could be included. If the problem is more extensive under some conditions than others, this characteristic also should be noted. For example, poverty is more widespread during periods of inflation and high unemployment.

The scope of the problem, including the number of people affected and the seriousness of the problem, should be presented. Also, this section should discuss whether the problem exists on a national, regional, community, or neighborhood level and at which level the policy will have an impact on the problem.

In policy analysis, if the policy problem has been described in limited or parochial terms, it has to be restated. For example, an analyst might be asked if guidelines mandating social workers in hospitals should be supported or opposed. This question could be restated to ask, "What is the effect of the number and the quality of human service workers on medical care?"[1]

Existing research and experience should be utilized when the problem is defined. There are many sources available for this work. It is possible to interview a few clients who are affected by the problem to get an in depth understanding of the problem. Or, a formal needs assessment can be undertaken. A sample of all of the clients can be questioned about the social problem. Social workers and others who work with clients affected by the problem can be consulted, as can educators in the area. There often is published material, such as books and articles by authorities and studies by local, regional, and national agencies, which can be helpful in defining the problem.

There should be evidence in this section that some of these sources were consulted and that the definition of the social problem is based on reality. The social problem should not be an assumed problem created by a policy maker.

Values. Is this an important problem?

Based on values, some problems seem more important than others. A list of social problems could be ranked in terms of relative importance. Since resources are scarce, policy makers constantly are making judgments about the relative importance of various social problems.

Social policies are not developed to affect social problems until there is general agreement by significant numbers of people that there is a social problem and that something should be done about the social problem.[2] In other words, social conditions may exist for a long time, without there being general agreement on the need to change them. At various times in our history, social problems such as poverty, illness, divorce, and delinquency have been seen as serious, and social policies have been developed for these social problems. At other times, these problems have received very little attention. Timing is extremely important in selecting social problems which are amenable to social policy intervention.

The selection of social problems for which policy will be created is in part based on values. Policy developers and analysts can determine whether the problem under consideration is a meaningful and important one in comparison to other social problems.

Politics. Is this definition of the problem politically feasible?

In addition to values, politics are important in determining whether a social problem will be seen as important.

Any policy must compromise between what is desirable and what is possible. In dealing with what is possible, issues of power and scarcity can be important. When there are extensive available resources and a proposed policy is perceived to benefit all the powerful individuals and interest groups, there is little conflict. However, in most cases, social policies are perceived to benefit one group while not benefiting or diminishing the power and/or resources of another group. In most cases, allocating resources to one social policy reduces resources available for other policies. In these instances, issues of power and economic efficiency become extremely important in determining policy choices.[3]

Many authors have commented on the importance of interest groups in the policy making process. Theodore Marmor, in his book *The Politics of Medicare*,[4] describes the organizational process model and the bureaucratic politics model of policy development. Under the organizational process model, the skill and power of interest groups are used to explain aspects of the development of the Medicare Program. Policy can be developed as a result of the interaction of interest groups. For the policy analyst, the organizational process model can be used to understand the effect of organizational behavior on policy. In the Medicare example, Marmor writes that groups such as the American Medical Association and the National Chamber of Commerce were initially opposed to national health insurance for the elderly. Labor Unions and senior citizens groups, among others, supported national health insurance for the elderly. All of these groups actively lobbied legislators. The resulting policy can be understood partly in terms of their power and skill in this process.

Powerful individuals, politicians, and bureaucrats also are significant in all phases of the policy process. Under the bureaucratic politics model, key actors become involved in order to benefit from the final outcome of the policy. Many of the actors have different conceptions of the problem, investments in different outcomes, and different terms upon which they will compromise. For Marmor, under this model, "where you stand depends upon where you sit."[5] The resulting policy is a "collage of individual acts, outcomes of minor and major games, and foul-ups."[6]

Policy can be understood therefore as the interaction of individuals and interest groups, who possess different degrees of skill and power and who are pursuing their own best interests or the best interests of their organizations and interest groups. These best interests may or may not coincide with the best interests of the clients or a rational policy based on research.

By describing individual and group politics, the policy analyst can understand and explain why a social problem was defined the way it was. The policy developer should try to anticipate individual and interest group pressures which will work to influence the definition of the problem, make some judgment about the skill and power of those who might support and those who might oppose the problem definition, and take these judgments into consideration as the policy is defined and developed.

Who Is Affected Directly by the Problem?

Research and Rationality. Is the description of the client group at the appropriate level of generality and consistent with existing research?

The client group should be described in terms of the commonalities among its members. Depending on the problem, categories such as age, sex, income, education, ethnicity, percentage of the population, and medical and psychological characteristics might be used. In addition, it is important to indicate whether the problem is primarily one of individuals, families, peer groups, or some combination of these units.

The level of generality at which the client group is defined is an important consideration in developing a policy. For example, the most general statement is that all citizens, or all those who reach a certain age, such as sixty-five, should receive some benefit. A still less general description of a client group might include all whose age is at least sixty-five and whose incomes fall below a given level. Another less general definition could identify the client group as poor elderly persons who are able to take care of themselves in the community, rather than requiring nursing home care.

Policies can be developed for all of the above client groups. It is important that the policy clearly defines the client population. The definition of the problem, the goals, and the programs to implement the policy should relate rationally to one another at the same level of generality. Obviously, a policy designed to support elderly persons in the community, so that they can stay out of nursing homes, should not have the goal of reducing poverty among all of the elderly in the country. This policy is directed toward only those elderly who are living in the community, not to all elderly.

A common mistake in policy development is to define the

client group broadly, such as all poor people, or all elderly, or all juvenile delinquents, and then not account for the differences within this population. The group poor people is composed primarily of women, children, and the elderly. While there are some policies which are needed for "all poor people," there are also very important differences between the needs of poor children, poor women, and poor elderly persons. Careful attention should be paid to whether the client group as defined is really the group which the policy will and should benefit.

Research is important in the identification of those who are affected directly by the problem. The policy should select a client group based on clear and defensible criteria and evidence.

Are the criteria used to select clients supported by research and rationality?

There are different ways to select clients for a policy. The most general distinction is between universal policies which identify clients on the basis of some universal status, such as age, and selective policies which serve clients on the basis of some specialized need, which occurs among a percentage of the population.

Neil Gilbert and Harry Specht have developed a more specific system of categorizing the basis upon which clients become eligible for social programs.[7] Their system includes the categories of attributed need, compensation, diagnostic differentiation, and means tested need.

For Gilbert and Specht, eligibility under attributed need is available to a category or group of people who have similar needs which are not being met by the marketplace. For example, society might decide, as has been done in many European countries, that there is a right to health care and that everyone should be eligible. Or, it might be decided that all working mothers have needs for day care which should be provided by the society. Benefits are provided as a right and on the basis of some universal or partially universal status.

Compensation provides benefits to those who have made some economic and social contribution to the society or who have had to suffer unfairly in society. For example, the United States has an extensive system of programs for veterans of foreign wars. It is felt that those who have fought for the country, and in some cases, have been injured, should be provided extra benefits. Also, if a group, such as women, or nonwhites, have been discriminated against unfairly, society may decide to compensate them through various social policies. Additionally, it is not unusual for society to provide benefits for individuals who have to move because they are in the path of some public improvement, such as a highway, which is to benefit the common good.

Diagnostic differentiation is practiced by human service professionals. To become eligible for a service under diagnostic differentiation, a client must be referred or admitted to a program by a professional. Eligibility for provisions is based on professional judgments. For example, the emotionally ill and the physically disabled often are admitted or not admitted to programs on the basis of diagnostic differentiation.

The last category is means tested need. Here, eligibility is based on evidence, usually furnished by the client, regarding his or her inability to purchase needed goods and services. Means tested need is most characteristic of public welfare programs.[8]

Values. What values are important in the selection of the client group? Are these appropriate values?

Along with research and rationality, and politics, values can influence the criteria which are used to select the client group. Universal or selective criteria can be used because policy makers think that these criteria are appropriate. Clients can become eligible for programs based on the model of attributed need, compensation, diagnostic differentiation, and/or means tested need. These principles are ranked in terms of whether provisions are seen as a right or whether their receipt carries with it some stigma. Generally speaking, attributed need and compensation are seen as rights. In the United States, they would include programs such as Social Security and Veterans Benefits. Diagnostic differentiation and means tested need tend to carry more stigma. Given the social problem, the policy analyst or policy maker should decide which criteria for selecting clients is used and whether it is appropriate.

Politics. What individuals and groups, if any, support and which ones oppose this definition of the client group? What effect, if any, does this have on the definition of the problem?

In addition to involving research and rationality and values, the definition of a social problem is a political act. Especially important in this respect is the determination of the composition of the client group. Some individuals and organizations may feel that the client group is too large and is defined too broadly. Other individuals and organizations may feel that they are being excluded unfairly from the potential benefits of the policy and may lobby to be included. For example, when the Model Cities program first was developed in the 1960s, it was seen as an experimental approach to community renewal in a few, selected American cities. However, once the program was made public, cities all across the country pressured Washington to expand the program so they could be included in it. This pressure was effective. What began as an experimental approach for a few cities quickly became a national program for all cities whose applications were acceptable.

Conversely, a policy proposed by President Truman to develop national health insurance was to include all Americans. This definition of the client group was defeated by powerful interest groups who felt that the policy would be too expensive and inconsistent with a free market ideology. Eventually, the decision was made to concentrate on one group, the elderly, as a client group who would receive benefits under the program. The poor were added later to the policy.

When problems and policies are discussed on the community, regional, state or national level, individuals and interest groups attempt to assess how they will be affected by these policies and act accordingly. If the individuals and interest groups feel that they will benefit from the policies, they will support or at the least not oppose them. If individuals and interest groups feel that they will not benefit from the policies or will be affected adversely, they may oppose these policies. Assessment and consequent action or inaction occur at all stages of the policy process.

How Was the Problem Caused?

Research and Rationality. Does the existing research support the cause(s)?

All policies make assumptions about how problems are caused. In most cases, these assumptions are not stated. The policy analyst usually will have to make inferences about the causes which the original policy makers ascribed to the problem. In policy development, it is important to think carefully and explicitly about causes since they affect the eventual policy.

There should be an examination of existing research and experience to determine what is known about how a social problem is caused. If the cause can be determined with precision, the selection of a program to solve the problem is easier.

Values. What values are important in determining the cause(s) of the problem? Are these appropriate values?

For many social problems, the research and theoretical literature propose more than one cause. There is often no rational or empirical way to choose one or more causes of a problem over another. Therefore, the policy analyst or policy developer must make a decision based on what seems right or is consistent with his or her general approach to social problems.

Generally speaking, causes of social problems can be seen to lie within the individual who has the problem, within one or more major features of a society, or within some combination of the two. Individualists feel that the individual is primarily responsible for the problem and develop policies aimed at helping or changing the individual. Collectivists attribute the cause of social problems primarily to societal institutions and favor policies which change these institutions. Those who believe that a given social problem has many different causes would develop a many faceted social policy.

For example, if the primary cause of child abuse is seen as a problem within the family unit, the resulting policy would seek to treat or strengthen the family. If child abuse were seen as occurring more often during times of high unemployment, efforts to change the type, location, and distribution of jobs would be favored. If an individual, such as a parent or a child, were seen as the main cause of abuse, policies would be directed to change this individual. A multifaceted social policy would emerge if policymakers felt there were multiple causes.

Values, along with research and rationality, are important in selecting the cause or causes of social problems. Since assumptions about causes are important in determining programs, causes should be dealt with explicitly in social policy. Both the policy analyst and the policy developer then can make judgments based on research and rationality and on values.

Politics. What effect, if any, do individuals and groups have on the selection of causes?

Powerful individuals and groups often develop orientations to social problems, including their causes. These orientations are consistent with the best interests of the individuals and groups. For example, job training agencies will assert that an important cause of unemployment is the lack of job training. They therefore will work to have their definition of the cause of unemployment accepted.

Politics can be important in assumptions about the causes of social problems in the absence of generally held research based determinations of social causes. Policy analysts and policy developers need to account for the effect of politics on the choice of a cause for a social problem.

SUMMARY

The definition of the social problem is extremely important. The remainder of the policy is built upon it. The way the problem is described, the selection of the clients, and the selection of the causes of the problem will have an effect on the resulting policy.

This chapter presented a detailed model for the first phase in the policy process, definition of the social problem. Specifically, the following areas were discussed.

What is the Social Problem?

> Research and Rationality. Is the definition of the social problem rational and consistent with existing research?

> Values. Is this an important problem?

> Politics. Is this definition of the problem politically feasible?

Who is Affected Directly by the Problem?

> Research and Rationality. Is this description of the client group at the appropriate level of generality and consistent with existing research? Are the criteria used to select clients supported by research and rationality?

> Values. What values are important in the selection of the client group? Are these appropriate values?

> Politics. What individuals and groups, if any, support and which ones oppose this definition of the client group? What effect, if any, does this have on the definition of the problem?

How Was the Problem Caused?

> Research and Rationality. Does the existing research support the cause(s)?

> Values. What values are important in determining the cause(s) of the problem? Are these appropriate values?

Politics. What effect, if any, do individuals and groups have on the selection of causes?

The next phase will present the detailed model for the second phase in the policy process, Implementation of the social policy.

NOTES

1. James J. Gallagher, Models for Policy Analysis: Child and Family Policy," In Ron Haskins & James J. Gallagher (eds.). *Models for Analysis of Social Policy: An Introduction.* Norwood, N.J.: Ablex Publishing Co., 1981, pp. 37–77.

2. Harry Gold & Frank Scarpitti, *Combating Social Problems: Techniques of Intervention.* New York: Holt, Rinehart & Winston, 1967, p. 2.

3. Joseph Heffernan, *Introduction To Social Policy: Power, Scarcity, and Common Human Needs.* Itasca, Ill: F.E. Peacock Pub. Inc., 1979, pp. 25–39.

4. Theodore Marmor, *The Politics of Medicare.* Chicago: Aldine Publishing Co., 1970.

5. *Ibid.*

6. *Ibid.*

7. Neil Gilbert & Harry Specht, *Dimensions of Social Welfare Policy.* N.J.: Prentice-Hall, Inc., 1974, pp. 66–68.

8. *Ibid.*

Chapter 14

IMPLEMENTATION OF THE SOCIAL POLICY

INTRODUCTION

This chapter presents the second phase of the model for analyzing and developing social policy, implementation of the social policy. In describing the implementation phase of a social policy, the following questions are asked?

What are the goals and objectives of the policy?

What provisions implement the policy?

What is the organizational structure of the administering agency?

How is the policy to be financed?

This chapter presents the implementation of the social policy in terms of the factors used throughout the model—research and rationality, values, and politics.

What Are the Goals and Objectives of the Policy?

Research and Rationality. Are the goals and objectives consistent with existing research and do they relate logically to the definition of the problem?

Goal statements relate to ideal end situations. Goals are what is to be accomplished. They are statements of general intent. For example, in policy for juvenile delinquency, the goal might be to reduce the rate of juvenile delinquency. Sometimes goal statements incorrectly include sections on means, or the ways the goals are to be accomplished. In the statement, "the goal of this policy is to reduce juvenile delinquency through counseling," only the first part of the statement, "to reduce juvenile delinquency," is, technically, a goal. Counseling is a program, and in the model it should be included under the programs section.

Policies can include objectives, in addition to goals. Goals are broad statements of purpose. Objectives are more specific and often are more amenable to measurement. A given goal can have more than one objective. For example, if the goal is to reduce juvenile delinquency, objectives might include, "to reduce the rate of first time offenders by 15 percent," "to reduce the rate of second and third time offenders by 10 percent," and "to reduce the rate of delinquent acts by youth, ages ten to fifteen by 10 percent."

Sometimes goals and objectives in a policy statement are not clear or do not appear to be realistic. The policy analyst then must develop goals and objectives. This work can be done in at least three ways. The policy analyst can predict the results of a particular policy and designate these results as goals and objectives. Or the analyst can establish goals and objectives and select a policy which is likely to attain them. Finally, the policy analyst can consider the stated goals and objectives as ideal, but probably not realistic, given other aspects of the policy. In this situation, it would not be necessary for the policy to accomplish exactly the stated goals and objectives.[1]

It is possible for policies to be internally inconsistent. The goals and the objectives might not make sense for the problem described and the client group identified. The program selected might not follow from the identified causes of the problem.

Since decisions about the identification of the client group, the goals and objectives of the policy, the causes of the problem, the program, the financing, and the organizational structure may be influenced by values and politics, it is possible that the resulting policy will not make rational sense. If the policy is illogical, major inconsistencies should be identified and alternatives suggested during consideration of the implementation plan.

Social policies can be designed either to treat an existing social problem and/or to prevent a social problem. A policy designed to prevent social problems is aimed at potential clients who might be vulnerable to a problem. In describing a policy's goals, a determination should be made about whether the purpose is primarily to prevent, to treat, or to do both.

Values. What values affect the goals and objectives? Are these values appropriate?

Values are extremely important in the selection of goals and objectives. For example, some policy makers, in considering the problem of poverty, have the goal of reducing the costs to society. Others concentrate on improving the conditions of clients. Similarly, some policy makers see juvenile delinquency as primarily a problem of social control. Their goals are to protect society and to punish those who break the law. From a different value orientation, a major goal in the area of delinquency could emphasize the rehabilitation of the individual youth.

The policy analyst should determine the major values which underlie the goals of a social policy. A judgment then can be made on the appropriateness of these goals, given the value orientation of the policy analyst. Similarly, the policy developer should carefully consider the values inherent in the goals of a proposed policy.

Politics. What are the relative levels of power of competing policies? How does this affect the policy?

Social policies are developed in a particular time and place and must be understood in their context. Social policies compete for scarce resources with other public policies. In addition, for resources allocated for social welfare, there is strong competition among different client groups. In considering a social policy, it is important either to account for or to predict the support that can be expected for the social policy, given the demands of other public policies and other social policies.

WHAT PROVISIONS IMPLEMENT POLICY?

Research and Rationality. What are the Provisions?

Provisions are what is actually provided by a social policy. Provisions can be distinguished from programs, which include specific provisions and the organizational structure necessary to deliver these provisions. Neil Gilbert and Harry Specht[2] describe specific types of provisions which social policies make available to clients. Their list of provisions is presented here, with some changes and additions.

Social policies can provide one or more of the following: goods, services, vouchers, opportunities, power, money, and planning and organization. Specific provisions can be distinguished in terms of the degree to which they are transferable. In other words, these provisions can be ranked in terms of the degree to which they allow for recipient choice.

Goods are concrete things, such as food, clothing, and housing. Goods also have been considered an in kind benefit. The actual food is provided instead of cash for buying food. The provision of goods reduces recipients' decision making power, and some policy makers feel it therefore increases dependency. This increase in dependency is said to occur because recipients usually have little opportunity to select the types of goods which are most suited to their needs.

Services are provisions which are carried out for recipients.

Specific examples include advocacy, counseling, information and referral, teaching, and healing. As with goods, the beneficiary has little ability to exchange one type of service for another.

Vouchers are provisions which can be exchanged for goods and services. One example is food stamps. Recipients buy stamps which can be used to purchase food at a discount. Giving vouchers allows recipients more freedom to decide than does giving goods. However, like services, vouchers restrict recipients to certain categories of provisions. Food stamps, for example, cannot be used to buy soap.

Opportunities can be provided for members of society who have been discriminated against or who need extra assistance. For example, governments may provide extra assistance and opportunities in hiring for veterans of American wars. More recently, educational institutions, government, and industry have provided extra opportunities in some cases for minority group members, women, and handicapped persons.

Provision of power involves the redistribution of power over the control of resources and goods. Redistributing power includes insuring that recipients have some influence over agencies which serve them by placing them on boards of directors. Policies which provide for the development of neighborhood organizations and interest groups or which help to encourage wider participation in public affairs provide power to recipients.

The provision of money benefits, as through Social Security or Public Assistance, provides the maximum transferability and decision making power for recipients. Cash also can be provided indirectly through the income tax system. For example, families can deduct money from their income tax bill for each of their children. There are deductions for other expenses as well, such as medical expenses and business expenses available to those who pay taxes.

Some policies do not provide specific benefits to clients, such as goods or cash. The purpose of these policies is to reorganize and repackage or coordinate and monitor programs. The trend toward merging conditional grants-in-aid into block grants is an example of this type of policy. The creation of regional planning bodies which review and must approve changes in a community delivery system is another example of a policy which is concerned more with the organization of the service delivery system than with the provision of specific programs to clients.

Most social policies either will involve a reorganization of the service delivery system or will provide specific benefits to clients, such as goods, services, vouchers, opportunities, power, or money. These categories are generally accepted categories which can be used to describe the provisions which are intended to implement a social policy.

Does the existing research support the provisions selected to implement the policy?

A social policy can make rational sense but not have support from research and from experience. To determine whether sufficient support exists, there should be a survey of the existing literature relating to program evaluation of similar type provisions. It also may be helpful to talk with workers who have had professional experience in working with those affected by the social problem. Clients also can be helpful in evaluating the effectiveness of provisions.

It is not unusual for policies to implement provisions which have failed in the past. This rejection of past experience occurs because values and politics are so important in implementation. Provisions are chosen which are consistent with societal values, and which therefore have a good chance of receiving legislative approval.

There is another reason why some policies have failed in the past. In America, as a result of pragmatism, policy makers tend to develop provisions before defining the problem carefully. If there is support for expansion of services to the elderly, for example, agencies will tend to propose expansion of existing provisions, whether they include counseling, group work, or community organization. Instead of starting with a careful definition of the problem and then developing a policy consistent with that definition, there is a strong predisposition to emphasize the implementation structure first. This American pragmatism, which emphasizes means, or provisions, over ends, or goals, can result in policies which are ineffective and inefficient. They tend to be agency centered rather than client centered. This agency centeredness occurs because prime consideration often is given to the provisions which agencies can deliver, rather than to provisions which clients need. It is not unusual, then, for research and experience to question existing or proposed policies and provisions.

Values. Does the policy treat clients appropriately in terms of equality, equity, adequacy, and client self-determination?

Equality, equity, and adequacy. Social policies can be assessed in terms of the degree to which they promote the values of equality, equity, and adequacy. Equality is concerned with the extent to which a policy involves redistribution of resources. Most selective policies, since they benefit one group and are paid for by others, result in some redistribution of resources. The redistribution usually is progressive, involving provisions for those in need which are paid for by those with relatively more resources (through voluntary contributions and/or through taxation). It is possible, of course, for social policies to have a proportional or regressive effect on the overall distribution of resources in the society. Generally, under proportional policies, contributors receive back roughly what they contributed. In regressive policies, people in need and lower income persons contribute a higher percentage of their resources than do higher income persons.

Some policies are concerned more directly with the value of equality than are others. For example, policies in the income maintenance area, such as those for poor families, clearly are related directly to the value of equality. Other policies, such as mental health policies, affect to some extent the overall distribution of resources in the society, but more indirectly than do income maintenance policies.

For Winifred Bell, equity is "the degree to which people in like circumstances and with similar needs are treated equally."[3] Equity is concerned with similar treatment of all those within the client group. It is felt that all those with similar needs should be treated equally. There should not be preferential treatment for some clients over others.

Equality is concerned with differences between the client group and the rest of society, whereas equity is concerned with relationships among clients. To work towards the goal of equality, a policy would involve some redistribution of resources from the general population to those in need. To work towards equity, a policy would treat all clients covered by the policy, or related policies, the same.

Adequacy is concerned with whether sufficient provisions are available to clients under the policy. The standard of adequacy can be applied to all provisions which directly benefit clients. One can ask whether the grant available to clients under AFDC is adequate or whether the amount and quality of services which clients receive from a family counseling agency are adequate. Adequacy is related to equality, since more adequate programs for those in need can be seen to promote more equality. The difference is that equality emphasizes the position of clients relative to the rest of society, while adequacy is concerned with whether the social policy is providing sufficient provisions to deal with the clients' problems.

Generally speaking, recent literature in social welfare and pronouncements of professional groups have favored social policies which promote equality and equity and are adequate. The degree to which a particular policy will strive to achieve these values depends on the values of policy makers and the political realities.

Social Control or Client Self-Determination. Policies which emphasize social control are concerned primarily with protecting society from problems caused by clients. Other policies emphasize the rights, responsibilities, and self-determination of clients and are not as concerned with the effect which clients can have on society. Finally, policies can include aspects of both social control and client needs. For example, placing criminals in prisons is primarily a social control policy. It has been shown in other countries that there are alternative methods of helping many criminals to change their behavior which are more effective and less expensive than prisons in reducing crime. Given the goals and objectives of the policy, a value judgment can be made regarding the relative importance of social control or clients' needs.

Specific provisions can be selected which emphasize social control or client self-determination.[4] In other words, some provisions are more transferable than others. Clients have more freedom and decision making ability with provisions which are transferable.

In our society, money is the most transferable provision. Policies which provide money give clients the most ability to control their own lives. In contrast, goods and services are more difficult to transfer. Counseling, for example, cannot be exchanged for something else. Vouchers, such as food stamps, provide some transferability. A client must use the stamps for food. His or her freedom lies in making decisions about the kinds of food to be purchased.[5]

Where clients are relatively competent, there should be provisions which provide a high degree of transferability. As much as possible, the goal should be to increase client independence through the exercise of decision making. In cases where a client's independence could have serious negative consequences, less transferable programs should be implemented.

Whether provisions are transferable or not is related to politics also. In part because of our Poor Law inheritance, policy makers have been more willing to provide in kind benefits, such as goods and services, than cash, which has a high transferability value.

Politics. Is there sufficient support to give the policy a reasonable chance of being acted upon?

Social policies vary over time in their popularity and political support. During the 1960s, there was strong support for developing new approaches to a variety of social policies. During the 1970s and 1980s, broad public support for social policies has weakened. This weakening has affected policies which were developed during the 1960s and proposed policies. The policy analyst, in trying to understand the composition of an existing social policy, must take into account the social climate and especially the politics. The policy developer works at creating a new policy in a political context which affects all aspects of the policy process.

There are some policies which are more popular and therefore have more political support than others. Sheila Kammerman and Alfred Kahn[6] have identified social policies in relation to the amount of public support which they enjoy. Kammerman and Kahn feel that strong support exists for policies which are needed for the everyday living of "normal" people. Examples are public education, public health, and retirement and survivors' benefits available under Social Security. These are policies which individuals cannot provide for themselves and are important for society. They are essentially universal type programs.

There is ambivalence towards policies for special groups which have unique problems and needs. These policies are organized because individual provision of these services in not practical. These policies also are for needs which most people might experience, although only some actually do experience. Specific examples are programs for the aged, private family counseling programs, community centers and settlement houses, and programs for veterans. Policies for special groups are somewhere between universal and selective type policies.

Finally, Kammerman and Kahn observe that there are policies which elicit negative feelings from the public, and therefore, less political support. These policies are approached with Poor Law attitudes. Those in need of help are blamed for their problem. Clients are seen as inadequate. These policies often try to control clients or to treat them punitively. These policies often are staffed or financed poorly. Examples are Aid to Families with Dependent Children (AFDC), Antipoverty Programs, Food Stamps, housing programs for the poor, correctional facilities, and state mental hospitals. These are selective type policies available on the basis of need. Kammerman and Kahn feel that the result of this varying public support is the development of social service networks based on class. Middle and upper class persons make more use of programs which have strong or moderate support, and lower class persons use programs which have little public support.[7]

Support for particular goals and social programs usually is strongly political. The policy analyst and the policy developer must consider the amount of political support for a particular social policy implementation approach.

WHAT IS THE ORGANIZATIONAL STRUCTURE OF THE ADMINISTRATING AGENCY?

Research and Rationality. Is the organizational structure appropriate for the policy?

How programs are organized and administered can be as important to final success as what is provided. To the extent possible, this section should describe the organizational structure which makes social programs available to clients.

Human service agencies can be described in terms of their organization, their size and complexity, and the qualifications and abilities of their staff.

Social service organizations which are established by social policies to deliver social provisions can be either governmental organizations, private organizations, or some combination of the two. Some programs, such as Social Security and Public Assistance are provided wholly by government. Other services, such as group services for teenagers and family counseling, tend to be provided by privately supported agencies. However, many private agencies may receive some public funds through grants and contracts and through insurance payments. Many public agencies contract for service with private agencies. A description of the organizational structure should begin with a determination of whether the agency which will deliver the services is a public agency, a private agency, or some combination of the two.

Social service organizations usually do not have the autonomy of business enterprises. This relative lack of autonomy occurs because social service agencies usually are not self-sufficient in their funding. Support typically comes from the community, either through voluntary donations to charity or through taxes levied by government. Since these organizations are not economically self-sufficient, the broader community usually demands a role in the decision making process. In the private sector, social agencies have boards of directors which represent important community interests. In the public sector, various types of control are exerted by governmental officials over the delivery of public social services. The degree of autonomy which a human service agency has in making decisions can have an important effect on program.

A part of the description of the agency or organization should deal with the type of control over agency operations, whether by a private board of directors or by a government bureau. In public organizations, it would be useful to determine if the model of control is similar to the conditional grant-in-aid, the block grant, or the totally decentralized control characteristic of General Revenue Sharing. Since social programs rarely are self-sufficient, the type of control exerted over their operation can have a major impact on their effectiveness.

Size has been found by researchers to be an extremely important predictor of many aspects of an organization's functioning. Generally speaking, larger organizations tend to be more bureaucratic, have more formal rules, and be less flexible. Top administrators and/or the board of directors make most of the major decisions. Other agencies, especially smaller, decentralized organizations with a high proportion of professional staff, work more on a collegial model, with shared decision making on the basis of professional judgment.[8]

Many human service organizations, especially in the public sector, have organizational units in different communities across the country. When this decentralization occurs, the size of the organizational units should be described, along with the degree of autonomy of the organizational unit from the central organization.

Finally, the numbers, qualifications, and abilities of the staff are extremely important in delivering social service provisions. To the extent possible, information on the staff also should be presented under this section.

Basically the question is whether the organizational structure is appropriate, given the goals of the policy. On the basis of existing experience, research, and values, is the organization of the appropriate size, and is it staffed with the people qualified to accomplish the goals of the policy? Are the internal decision making structure and the system of power and control within the organization appropriate?

Until recently, there has been relatively little attention given to the organization and administration of agencies which implement social policy. Now there is a growing body of literature and experience regarding organization size, structure, decision making, and staffing which can be used in program development and analysis.

Values. Will the organizational structure promote efficient and effective service delivery?

There has been increasing concern about issues of efficiency and effectiveness in social policy. These are legitimate questions which need to be addressed. Efficiency deals with the best utilization of organizational resources, such as money, staff, energy, and time, in order to decrease waste. Effectiveness deals with the best arrangement of organizational components in order to accomplish the goals and objectives of a policy.

Although related, efficiency and effectiveness are different. It would be possible to have a very efficient organizational structure, with minimal waste, which was not effective in meeting the goals and objectives of the policy. Similarly, it would be possible for an organization to exert significant impact on a social problem, but to waste money, staff, energy, and/or time in the process.

Organizational structure is an important determinate of both efficiency and effectiveness. Therefore, the policy developer and the policy analyst must consider whether the proposed or existing organizational structure maximizes the values of efficiency and effectiveness.

Politics. What individuals and groups benefit from this policy? Who loses? What effect does this have on implementation?

Support and opposition also exist at the stage of program selection. If anything, contending forces are more active during this stage. Individuals, agencies, clients, and interest groups, depending on their power and skill, can have a major effect on the policy. Often their efforts bear little relationship to the rational needs of the client group as identified in the problem definition section. To understand why a policy developed the way it did, or to implement a new policy, careful attention must be paid to forces which support and oppose the program.

In policy analysis, it is sometimes possible to understand how a policy was changed because of the influence of individuals and groups. Theodore Marmor, for example, suggests that doctors agreed not to oppose actively a federally sponsored medical care policy for the elderly if the federal government would not regulate the procedures doctors could undertake or the fees they could charge under the Medicare program.[9]

In policy development, an assessment of the political situation is crucial to success. Given the political climate, often it is not possible to implement the exact policy which was envisioned. At times, the basic policy can be kept intact, and compromises can be made regarding the language used in the policy and the groups which will implement the policy. At other times, more basic changes must be made to gain the support necessary to implement a social policy. In some cases, the policy developer may decide that the benefits of the policy outweigh the negative aspects of the changes and that the policy therefore should be pursued. In other cases, the policy developer could conclude that the changes which need to be made in order to get sufficient political support are so destructive to the policy that it should not be pursued.

Under a democracy, policy of all kinds goes through numerous changes as it first is proposed and then is implemented. The resulting policy is always a compromise between various rational, value, and political considerations. Sometimes the compromises are so great that the policy is ineffective, inefficient, or counterproductive. Both the policy analyst and the policy developer should approach their task knowing that there are almost no social policies which do not change during the phases of policy development.

How Is the Policy to Be Financed?

Research and Rationality, Values and Politics. Is financing adequate, predictable, and provided in the proper form?

An important aspect of a social policy is the method which will be used to finance the social programs. Policies can be financed by one or more of the various levels of government. Policies can be financed, wholly or partly, by the private sector. Financing can be accomplished through user fees, contributions, or grants from the United Way, foundations and other organizations.

There are three aspects of financing which will be addressed here. A major question is whether, based on past and present experience, the financing is adequate to achieve the goals of the policy. Adequacy of financing is a serious concern. Money for social policies has become less available despite the continued growth of serious social problems. The lack of adequate financing can be as detrimental to achieving the goals of a policy as can a poorly conceived policy. Research and the experience of other programs can indicate high and low limits, or thresholds, for financing. Values and politics are also extremely important.

A second major question related to financing is the term for which the financing is available. Given the goals of the policy, what is a reasonable time period of program implementation for results to be evident? It is not unusual for programs to be funded for an extremely short term. The result of this short term funding is that administrators and staff may need to devote an inordinate amount of time and energy to securing alternative funds. Insufficient time and energy may remain for implementing the policy.

204 SOCIAL POLICY IN AMERICAN SOCIETY

The form in which monies are distributed and the amount of control which is attached to these monies should be considered also. There are three basic forms of control which have been discussed earlier. Under the conditional grant-in-aid, the funding body controls both the goals and the means of a policy. Under the block grant form, the funding body controls the goals and the administering agency controls the means of a policy. Finally, under the General Revenue Sharing type of grant, the administering agency controls the goals and the means of the policy, with the funding body merely distributing the money. These forms have developed under federalism in the public sector but are applicable to grants to private agencies also. While they were discussed earlier in terms of the federal government's relationship to the states and localities, the grant-in-aid, block grant, and General Revenue Sharing forms are applicable to relationships between funding bodies and recipient agencies on all levels.

This chapter has presented implementation of the social policy in terms of research and rationality, values and politics. Following is an outline of this part of the model.

What are the Goals and Objectives of the Policy?

Research and Rationality. Are the goals and objectives consistent with existing research and do they relate logically to the definition of the problem?

Values. What values affect the goals and objectives? Are these values appropriate?

Politics. What are the relative levels of power of competing policies? How does this affect the policy?

What Provisions Implement the Policy?

Research and Rationality. What are the provisions? Does the existing research support the provisions selected to implement the policy?

Values. Does the policy treat clients appropriately in terms of equality, equity, adequacy, and client self-determination?

Politics. Is there sufficient support to give the programs a reasonable chance of being acted upon?

What is the Organizational Structure of the Administering Agency?

Research and Rationality. Is the organizational structure appropriate for the policy?

Values. Will the organizational structure promote efficient and effective service delivery?

Politics. What individuals and groups benefit from this policy? Who loses? What effect does this have on implementation?

How is the Policy to be Financed?

Research and rationality, values, and politics. Is financing adequate, predictable, and provided in the proper form in terms of research and rationality, values, and politics?

Notes

1. Duncan, MacRae, Jr., & Ron Haskins, Models for Policy Analysis. In R. Haskins & J.J. Gallagher. (eds.), *Models for Analysis of Social Policy: An Introduction.* Norwood, N.J.: Ablex Publishing Co., 1981, p. 28.

2. Neil Gilbert, & Harry Specht, *Dimensions of Social Welfare Policy.* Englewood Cliffs, New Jersey: Prentice-Hall, 1970.

3. Winifred Bell, Analytic Tools that are Useful in Evaluating Social Welfare Programs. *Council on Social Work Education,* 1970, mimeo, p. 2.

4. Gilbert and Specht, *ibid.*

5. *Ibid.*

6. Sheila B. Kammerman, & Alfred J. Kahn, *Social Services in the United States: Policies and Programs.* Philadelphia: Temple University Press, 1976.

7. *Ibid.*

8. Nicos P. Mouzelis, *Organization and Bureaucracy: An Analysis of Modern Theories.* Chicago: Aldine Publishing Co., 1967.

9. Theodore Marmor, *The Politics of Medicare.* Chicago: Aldine Publishing Co., 1973.

Chapter 15

CONSEQUENCES OF THE SOCIAL POLICY

INTRODUCTION

This chapter completes the presentation of the Policy Analysis–Policy Development Model. The chapter describes the Policy Analysis–Policy Development Model for the last phase of social policy, the consequences of social policy. The model for the consequences of social policy asks the following questions:

What are the costs and benefits of the policy?

What are the consequences of the policy for the clients, the social system, and the social service system?

WHAT ARE THE COSTS AND BENEFITS OF THE POLICY?

Research and Rationality, Values and Politics. Are the costs and benefits appropriate in terms of research and rationality, values, and politics?

Cost has become one of the most important parts of any social policy. More recently, with the use of cost-benefit analysis, there have been efforts to identify benefits to recipients at different levels of costs. Cost-benefit analysis can be used both in policy analysis and in policy development.

Cost-benefit analysis involves the systematic study and comparison of the costs and benefits of alternative programs which might be implemented in some future time period. Cost-benefit analysis usually is undertaken in an environment of uncertainty. Because there are so many imponderables, cost-benefit analysis is rarely definitive, but it can assist decision makers. It tends to contribute more rationality to the decision making process.

There are two basic approaches to cost-benefit analysis. With the fixed utility method, alternative programs to accomplish a given objective are examined. The fixed budget approach assumes a given cost and attempts to determine the best way to maximize an objective.[1]

The concept of marginalism is important in cost-benefit analysis. Most budget decisions are concerned with spending a little more or a little less. Decisions then need to be made about the consequences for the benefits of a policy if there are relatively small increases or decreases in cost.[2] Further, there often is a point where an increase in costs is not associated with the same degree of increase in benefits. For example, it might be decided that benefits justify the cost of one school social worker for an elementary school. However, the probability would be high for diminishing returns in providing several school social workers full time to the same school. The benefits of the second and third school social worker might not justify the costs. Their services might be used more efficiently at other schools.[3]

Cost-benefit analysis attempts to make policy decisions more rational. In social welfare, however, there are many technical problems which detract from too heavy a reliance on this method.[4] A prime strength of cost-benefit analysis is that it emphasizes efficiency. However, in the process, it can ignore questions of effectiveness. For example, using cost-benefit analysis, several day care centers could be compared in terms of costs. Using efficiency criteria, the least expensive would be selected. However, the quality and therefore the effectiveness of the center selected might be very low. This possibility could not be evaluated with the use of a strict cost-benefit approach.

There are other drawbacks to cost-benefit analysis. Since the method is very complex, it tends to be applied to existing small scale programs rather than to major reform policies. This is because data are more readily available for existing programs. In addition, new policies often are inefficient at the beginning until administrators learn from experience. Consequently, costs are relatively high for newer policies when they are compared to existing programs. Cost-benefit analysis tends to favor existing policies over new ones.

In social welfare, it is often difficult to assign a numerical value to a benefit. How does one quantify, for example, increased happiness which can result from counseling? This is an additional difficulty when cost-benefit analysis is applied to social welfare.

Finally, because of the complexity of the factors involved, it is often difficult to demonstrate that a particular social policy results in a given benefit. We are not always sure, for example, of the specific effect of several counseling interviews, separate from all of the other things which are going on in a person's life. It often can be difficult to prove that an identified benefit resulted from a particular cost.

Cost-benefit analysis may help in making decisions, but it should not be relied upon totally in social policy. As Carl Buxbaum writes, "The tools for pursuing efficient resource allocations are more artistic than scientific. For economic analysis to work well, wise decision makers must fill in where science fails and noneconomic values are present. They must add reason, judgment, and humanitarian concern."[5]

WHAT ARE THE CONSEQUENCES OF THE POLICY FOR THE CLIENTS, THE SOCIAL SYSTEM, AND THE SOCIAL SERVICES SYSTEM?

Research and Rationality and Values. What are the intended and unintended consequences of the policy?

Clients. When costs and benefits are considered, they usually are estimated in terms of positive results of the policy. There can be negative consequences as well. Negative consequences usually are unintended or unforseen, (although all unintended consequences are not negative). There are instances of social policies which have created serious problems for clients. For example, for a long time, men were not allowed to receive help under the Aid to Families with Dependent Children Program. Therefore, if a man could not find work and could not support his family, he was forced to leave the family so that his wife and children could get financial help. This provision encouraged the breakup of low income families.

It is well known that sending young adults to jail often fosters a life of crime. Because of the importance of peer groups, youths in jail often learn how to break the law more effectively and adopt the value from other delinquents that illegal behavior is attractive. While they are removed from society for a period of time, this approach does not seem to have positive results for many youths who could be rehabilitated or for society in general.

These examples are just two of many examples in which social policy has had strong negative effects upon clients and the social system. A policy may be passed with the best of intentions. However, in most cases, very little or no attention is given to the negative consequences of the policy for the clients.

Social System. Social policies can have consequences for the social system as well. The social system is composed of all of the institutions, such as the family, schools, and government, and of societal values, such as freedom and equality, which make up society.

When developing a policy, little attention usually is paid to the consequences of the policy for the general social system. Systems theory assumes that human organization and institutions relate to each other in a more or less orderly fashion. Under systems theory, the social system is analogous to a complex organism, with each part related to the other. A change in one part has consequences for the other parts. For example, in the environment, as people have burned more fossil fuels and driven more automobiles, the atmosphere has become polluted. This pollution has resulted in negative consequences for human and animal health. Breathing is impeded and lung-related diseases have increased. Plant life also is affected negatively. A change in one part of the system affects all other parts.

While the systems model of the social system is an ideal, it often is not duplicated fully in reality. Sometimes, all of the parts of the system do not relate to each other harmoniously. In fact, it was shown in Chapter 3 that one function of social policy is to reduce the problems created in a complex social system when some of the parts—the institutions and values—are out of harmony.

Social policies can have important consequences for the social system. The Great Society programs of Lyndon Johnson helped to reduce inequality in the society while at the same time increasing social stability. A major increase or decrease in the amount of resources allocated to mental health can have consequences for the family, business, the economy, and the system of formal social control. While often created or changed in isolation from other public policy, social policy is related to the major values and institutions in society. It is very important to consider both the positive and the negative consequences which social policy can have on aspects of the social system.

Social Services System. The social services system is composed of individuals and organizations which deliver social welfare services. Family counseling agencies, mental health clinics, public welfare departments, school social workers, and residential treatment centers are examples of agencies which are part of the social service system.

The system of social provisions in most American communities rarely approaches being a complete system. Often, there are gaps in services, duplication of effort, and difficulties in the coordination of related services. For example, there might not be enough foster homes for all children in need. They are forced into institutions which are inappropriate. Clients released from state mental institutions might not find supportive services in their home community and therefore have trouble functioning outside of an institution. Since individual problems tend to be multifaceted and social service agencies tend to be specialized, there might be complications in the coordination of two or more agency services addressing the complex problems of a client or a group of clients.

Both proposed and existing social policies have consequences for the organization of the delivery of services on the community level. These consequences need to be considered.

Neil Gilbert and Harry Specht have developed four goals for the delivery of services on the community level.[6] They feel that the service system should be continuous, integrated, accessible, and accountable. However, the accomplishment of some of these goals may conflict with the implementation of others.

A continuous social service system is one in which all the services in a particular field, such as child welfare, are related to one another in a reasonable manner. Two clients with the same problem would receive the same services in a continuous system. In addition, there is a continuum of care, including out-patient care, intermediate or halfway-house care, and institutionalization. The needed and appropriate services are available in the proper amounts.

An integrated social service system is one in which the different fields of service are well related to one another. Many clients have complicated problems which require attention from more than one part of the social service system. A client might have financial problems requiring public assistance, a behavioral problem requiring attention from the corrections system, and a problem with addiction, requiring help from agencies that treat chemical dependency. In an integrated social service system, it would be possible to organize all of the different relevant services in these diverse fields to help the client.

The concept of continuity of care is concerned with insuring an adequate and logical sequence of services within a given social service field of practice. The concept of integration of services is concerned with coordinating services between fields of practice.

Integration of a social service system and continuity of a social service system are based on a systems model, in which every part relates to the whole. Each service has an important relationship to other services in the same field of service and in other fields of service. Changes in the basic demands and needs for service in one area affect services in other areas. For example, a decline in the institutionalization of persons with mental health problems should lead to an increase in service by group homes, family counseling agencies and mental health clinics. To the extent that they are possible to achieve, the integration and continuity of services are enhanced by centralized rational planning and coordination. A small group of experts, committed to the best interests of the clients, needs to make decisions about the most effective and efficient form for the social service system. As more and more individuals and agencies become involved in the planning process, each pursues its individual needs and the needs of its constituency. These separate pursuits of individual agencies might not coincide with the overall goal of an integrated and continuous social service system.

Yet, as the social service system becomes more centralized and bureaucratized, it tends to become less flexible. The social service system tends to provide services for the greatest number of people and is less able to take into account differences among clients and among neighborhoods and communities. This decreased flexibility can have the effect of making the service system less accountable and less accessible. Accountability concerns responsiveness to the needs of clients and the community in general. Accessibility means easy availability of a service. Accessibility can be thought of in both physical and psychological terms. If agencies are easy to get to, they are accessible. If a potential client feels comfortable going to an agency for service, the service is accessible.

Generally speaking, more decentralized, community based, and independent services tend to be accountable and accessible. Accountability and accessibility are enhanced when clients or their representatives are on the board of directors of agencies.

Locale influences accessibility and accountability. When a social worker regularly works in the neighborhood, like a public health worker, the services tend to be more accessible and accountable. Similarly, locating the neighborhood service center or family agency branch in the area it serves tends to increase accessibility and accountability. In contrast, a social agency which is geographically distant from its clients, is in an imposing building, and has an involved intake procedure may discourage many clients. However, small community social agencies, while they promote the values of accountability and accessibility, tend to fragment the total social service system. Since control is decentralized, agencies can change on short notice with little regard for the effects of these changes on the total system. While often responsive to a local community or interest group, small agencies may not fit rationally into the total social service system.

The goals of continuity and integration of services are concerned with the total social service system and the relationship of its parts. Often, when continuity and integration are emphasized, decisions are centralized and can be authoritarian. The goals of accessibility and accountability are concerned with the needs of particular groups of clients and agencies, irrespective of the total social service system. A service system which emphasizes accountability and accessibility can be very decentralized in its decision making. The difference is between centralized decisions based on rationality and research, in the ideal case, and decentralized decisions characteristic of a pluralist society and based rather on values and politics. The existing service system in most communities has contradictory patterns toward continuity and integration on the one hand and accessibility and accountability on the other.

A social policy can be characterized in terms of whether it enhances the goals of service integration and continuity or of accessibility and accountability. Further, a value judgment can be made about whether, given the overall goal of the policy, the service delivery goals of continuity and integration or of accountability and accessibility should be emphasized.

Politics. How do support and opposition to the policy at the community level affect the delivery of services?

Opposition which was expressed to a policy during its formulation may continue once a program is implemented. New opposition also can develop once a program is in place in a community and can have consequences for the policy. For example, many individuals and groups opposed parts of the Poverty Program and worked against it during its implementation phase. This opposition had serious consequences for the program and resulted eventually in changes in the Poverty Program. City mayors, for example, felt threatened because they were excluded from the program. Through political pressure, they succeeded in having the law changed so that they could exert more control over the program. The next major program for cities, Model Cities, gave almost total control to the mayors.

Programs also attempt to develop political support on the community level once they are in operation. This effort often involves significant amounts of time and energy. The use of agency resources to develop political and financial support is essential for social welfare programs whose existence is dependent on the community and government rather than on client fees.

In policy analysis, it is possible to determine the support and opposition a program generates and to describe the effects of each on the program. In policy development, it is possible to anticipate some of the support and opposition and to plan accordingly.

SUMMARY

In summary, the last part of the policy analysis–policy development model deals with consequences of the social policy. Major aspects of the consequences section are:

What are the Costs and Benefits of the Policy?

Research and rationality, values, politics. Are the costs and benefits appropriate in terms of research and rationality, values, and politics?

What are the Consequences of the Policy for the Clients, the Social System, and the Social Service System?

Research and rationality and values. What are the intended and unintended consequences of the policy? Politics. How do support and opposition to the policy at the community level affect the delivery of services?

Most social policies solve some problems and create others. It usually is not possible to find the perfect policy. Discussion of the positive and negative consequences is crucial to developing policies which are efficient and effective. Analyzing the consequences of social policies for the clients, the social services system, and the social system, is probably the most neglected area of policy development.

NOTES

1. Gene Fisher, The Role of Cost-Utility Analysis in Program Budgeting. In Fremong J. Lyden & Ernest G. Miller (eds.). *Planning-Programming-Budgeting: A Systems Approach to Management.* Chicago: Rand McNally, 1972, pp. 265–281.

2. Steven E. Rhoads, Economist and Policy Analysis. *Public Administration Review,* March, 1978, pp. 112–120.

3. W. Joseph Heffernan, *Introduction to Social Welfare Policy: Power, Scarcity and Common Human Needs.* Itasca, Ill.: F.E. Peacock Publishers, Inc., 1979, p. 81.

4. Carl B. Buxbaum, Cost-Benefit Analysis: The Mystique Versus the Reality. *Social Service Review,* September 1981, p. 468.

5. *Ibid.*

6. Neil Gilbert & Harry Specht, *Dimensions of Social Welfare Policy.* Englewood Cliffs, NJ: Prentice-Hall, Inc., 1974, pp. 107–135.

Part V:

NEW DIRECTIONS IN
SOCIAL POLICY

Chaper 16

SOCIAL POLICY AND THE FUTURE

INTRODUCTION

Social policy undergoes several transitions during the development of societies. As resources grow with industrialization, societies begin to meet social needs. One of the first results is that more young people survive. The increase in the number of children and youth puts pressure on institutions such as the schools. Eventually, the birth rate declines, and the population becomes older. The elderly become a political force and press for more expensive social programs, such as social security and health insurance. In addition, as the social welfare bureaucracy grows, it can become entrenched, and it can work for the expansion of social policy.[1] Growing economies can support the increased social welfare effort. However, when the rate of industrial growth decreases, both the interest in social policy and the ability to support policy efforts decrease. Generally speaking, "welfare growth follows material growth, and welfare slowdown follows economic slowdown."[2]

Social welfare always will be an essential institution in American society. However, it is constantly changing. The variations in

social policy are based on changes in the demographic base of
the society, changes in the economic growth rate, and changes in
the type and strength of political support for social welfare.[3]

DEMOGRAPHIC TRENDS

Social welfare policies respond to changes in the demographic base of society. In Chapter 2, demographic changes over the
past 10 or more years were presented in order to describe the
composition of the population. At present, Americans tend to
live in urban areas and surrounding suburbs. The population has
a higher percentage of both older people and poorer people
than it did in the past. There are more single-parent families
and more individuals who are choosing to live alone. The percentage of women who now are working has increased dramatically, as have the percentages of minority and foreign born
Americans. These changes have led to an increase, over the past
years, in social policies to help the elderly, the cities, families,
individuals with mental health problems, and the poor.

In addition to describing past changes, demographers can
predict population developments which can influence the social
policies of the future. Some of the existing trends are expected
to continue. It is felt that the population will continue to get
older, and there will be a need for policies for the elderly. Experts predict that women will continue to participate, at an increasing rate, in the labor force, with consequences for the functioning of both the family and the workplace. The proportion of
the population in poverty has been increasing in recent years.
This trend may continue, as groups in need compete for scarce
government resources and as the workplace becomes increasingly automated. Automation of manufacturing and of office
work has the potential to displace large numbers of workers.

Because of the postwar baby boom, demographers expect a
rise in the numbers of people seeking to increase their social
mobility. For the next 10 or so years, there will be increased competition for jobs among women, minority group members, and
people born in the late 1940s and early 1950s. This increased

competition will create the need for new social policies in the areas of training and retraining, as jobs require higher levels of skills. Social policies also might be needed to manage some of the social tensions created by a large number of people looking for jobs in a rapidly changing employment market.

During the latter part of the 1980s, demographers expect the population to comprise fewer teenagers and young adults. This trend could reduce the level of teenage unemployment, juvenile delinquency, and the need for some social policies directed towards youth. Towards the end of this century, it is expected that there will be a lack of workers to fill the available jobs.[4]

There has been a well documented shift of the population from the Northeast and Midwest to the newer sunbelt communities in the West, South, and Southwest. Many of those who moved found jobs in the military and technological economy. However, those who stayed behind are unemployed or are working in older manufacturing industries with uncertain economic prospects. This demographic shift has implications for changes in the type and location of social provisions. There also has been a shift of political power to these new communities with their more conservative and individualistic orientations.

ECONOMIC TRENDS

Economic projections also are important in predicting the shape of social welfare in the future. Clearly, certain social welfare provisions require minimal levels of support to ensure the orderly functioning of society. However, there are economic limits to the ability of a society to expand its tax-based contributions to social policy.

Many writers believe that the past economic growth will not continue.[5] Paul Blumberg writes that the growth of the American economy is hampered by a "permanent war economy" which, since the end of the Second World War, has drained significant economic and human resources away from productive investment. Further, the traditional American advantage in technology is being neutralized by rapid growth in other countries' technological expertise. Many of the newer industrial nations, with more efficient factories, may be able to surpass the United States, with its older industrial base.

During the past forty years, the United States was rich enough to afford large military expenditures along with growth in social welfare. According to Blumberg, ". . . as America becomes a poorer country, the arms race on the same postwar scale can be pursued only by making deep inroads into already languishing public services and social programs, and into private living standards as well."[6]

According to Lester Thurow,[7] the economy of the 1980s will have to deal with the problems of energy, slow economic growth, environmental problems, and regulation. Solving these economic problems will require certain groups in our society to suffer. For Thurow, the economy is like a zero-sum game. Without a growing gross national product, a decision to increase by a certain percentage of the GNP our investment in industrial plant and equipment will require a deduction identical in amount from some other group in the society. If some group gains, some other group must lose in a like amount.

In the past, in the absence of many of these economic problems, we have not had to offset gains with losses. As the pie increased in size, everyone, more or less, could benefit. But the pie is no longer growing at the same rate, and priorities must be established.

There is some indication that economic inequality is increasing in the society. This increase comes in part because more middle and upper class women are working and taking jobs from low-income workers. In the past, social welfare programs have helped to lessen the inequality inherent in the system. This trend will not continue. As Thurow writes, "We are entering a period of rising inequality where conventional income transfer programs will be incapable of preserving the current degree of inequality."[8]

As we work on the problems of coping with slow economic

growth, conserving and finding new sources of energy, and protecting the environment, some groups are going to benefit, and some are going to lose. Those most at risk are those most in need, the least powerful members of the society. A major task and a major challenge of social policy in the future will be to attempt to protect and support the losers in the emerging conflict over the distribution of scarce benefits.

POLITICAL TRENDS

Along with demographic and economic assumptions, it is important to make projections about politics. In the future, will there be powerful political coalitions willing to support increases in social policy? Labor unions, which in the past were major supporters of social policy advances, are becoming weaker and more concerned with protecting the jobs of their members, against the inroads of minorities and women. As the membership becomes more middle class, labor unions are unlikely to support measures for the needy as strongly as they have in the past.

Politics have changed also because of a revolution in the way in which information is collected and disseminated. The growth of the mass media, especially television, has had a significant impact on the structure of politics. Television has the effect of simplifying complex issues. Since time is expensive, television news often is similar to a headline service. This tendency to simplify favors candidates who offer quick and simple solutions to complex problems. This quality of television causes problems for social welfare. Most social problems are not amenable to simple solutions. Values and politics, instead of research and rationality, will continue to dominate social policy decisions if the communications media persist in emphasizing simplistic solutions to complex social problems.

In contrast to newspapers and news magazines, television communicates emotion better than facts. Since there always have been strong values and emotions associated with most social welfare problems, such as crime, child abuse, and public welfare, it may have become even harder to take a rational view of social policy. Quick, unthinking, emotional responses are likely to prevail. Finally, modern mass communications allow for more direct participation among voters. Television reaches a large audience, often on a very superficial level. Cube systems, through which viewers can be polled about their opinions on public issues, will be installed in more homes in the future. Large public surveys, such as those conducted by Harris and Roper, increase citizen participation. The decline of political parties and the development of special interest political groups have further eroded representative democracy. A result of this trend could be to give policy makers less flexibility in working for the common good of the total community as they strive to meet the individualistic interests of their powerful and vocal constituents.

The framers of the United States Constitution wanted representative democracy rather than direct democracy. They did not want a system of referenda where citizens voted immediately on every public issue. The founding fathers were wary of immediate emotional responses to complicated issues. Instead, the U.S. Constitution established a system of representative democracy. With representative democracy the decision making process is slowed down and therefore, hopefully, more thoughtful. The increasing democratization of public policy issues carries overtones of mob rule and may work against the best interests of minorities in American society.

SOCIAL POLICY IN AMERICAN SOCIETY

Social policy will react to changes in the demographic base of the society and to economic and political factors. In the past, social policies have expanded when the country has been faced with serious threats to the social, economic, and political systems. This expansion in response to need was true in the 1930s, when the problems associated with the Great Depression threatened capitalism and democracy. Again in the 1960s, the civil rights movement and the civil disturbances caused the government to expand social policy.

As social policy, along with economic policy, has been successful in solving or ameliorating some of the basic social problems, political support for continuing social policies has diminished. This decrease in support has occurred in part because some of those in need have been helped and are less vocal in their protests. Further, since social and economic policies have returned some stability to society, there is less pressure on the general population and on the leaders to support redistributive social policies. In a sense, successful social policies carry within them the seeds of their own destruction.

Whether expanding or contracting, social welfare is an essential function in society. Whether delivered by the federal, state, or local government, or by the private sector, social welfare services have existed since the beginning of modern civilization and will continue in the future.

In the United States, social welfare workers, by themselves, have not been powerful although they have been politically active.[9] Some observers conclude that social workers, since they are not autonomous, tend to follow existing ideology. As Paul Adams and Gary Freeman write, ". . . given the marginal class position of social workers and the ambiguous nature of their professional status, it is as likely that social workers will take on the political coloring of whatever coalition of economic and social forces is currently dominant."[10]

Social welfare workers who have basic professional commitments to the provision of effective and efficient services to clients will be unable to muster by themselves the political power necessary to protect and develop their social policies. To be effective, they must search out and join with other groups in the society, such as civil rights groups, some groups within organized religion, some groups within organized labor, client groups, and a few groups within the business community, for support for social welfare policy.

An overview of the history of social policy shows periods of expansion and periods of contraction. There are times of strong governmental involvement and times of activitiy by the private sector.

During the near term, there will not be significant increases or decreases overall in social welfare. Rather, ". . . we can expect contradictory pressures to expand and to contract social welfare."[11]

A rapid expansion of social policy does not seem imminent unless there is a major threat to the stability of the society, such as an economic depression or serious civil disturbances. The current American economy seems unable to support a dramatic increase in social welfare. Further, the decline in the numbers of children and youth in the population will diminish the need for expanded social welfare services for them. In the political arena, there is less support for expansion. Interest groups that previously supported growth in social welfare, such as labor unions, have lost power and are redirecting their resources towards coping with the immediate problems of their members.

However, there will be some pressures to increase expenditures for social welfare in the years ahead. As the elderly become a larger proportion of the population, their visibility and their political power will grow. As a result, support will grow for some expansion of social policies for the elderly. The difficulties of the American economy and the decline of blue collar jobs, especially in manufacturing, will continue to create serious human problems requiring governmental intervention. Finally, the severity of the social program cutbacks instituted by President Reagan and the resulting increase in inequality in American society will create counterpressures for some growth in social welfare.

Given this scenario, two major strategies should be pursued by human service workers concerned with improving social policies. An immediate task for social policy is to identify, support, and improve the most important social policies. Priorities must be established among social policies in terms of their effectiveness. In addition, particular attention should be given to the much neglected area of policy implementation. During a period of marginal increases in expenditures, social policies must be delivered in the most efficient manner.

The second strategy concerns the long range development

of social welfare policy. In the past, social workers and others have not been prepared with well developed proposals for the periods of major expansion in social policy. The result is that most social policy decisions have been made by economists, lawyers, and politicians. Social welfare workers have been left the task of implementing these policies and have been blamed when the policies were ineffective and inefficient. The long range social policy task is to research and develop social policies which can be presented once there is adequate political support for expanded social welfare efforts.

Notes

1. Leonard S. Miller, Determinants of the Welfare Effort: A Critique and Contribution. *Social Service Review*, March 1976, pp. 57–79.

2. Paul Terrell, Adapting to Austerity: Human Services After Proposition 13, *Social Work*, July 1981, p. 275.

3. Mayer Zald, Demographics, Politics, and the Future of the Welfare State. *Social Service Review*, March 1977.

4. Christopher Conte, Analysts Are Confident of Economic Health as the Decade Proceeds. *The Wall Street Journal*, September 14, 1981, p. 1.

5. Paul Blumberg, *Inequality in an Age of Decline*. New York: Oxford University Press, 1980.

6. *Ibid.*, p. xii.

7. Lester C. Thurow, *The Zero Sum Society: Distribution and the Possibilities for Economic Change*. New York: Basic Books, 1980.

8. *Ibid.*, p. 161.

9. James L. Wolk, Are Social Workers Politically Active? *Social Work*, July 1981, pp. 283–288.

10. Paul Adams & Gary Freeman, On the Political Character of Social Service Work. *Social Service Review*, December 1979, pp. 560–572.

11. George T. Martin, Social Welfare Trends in the United States, in George T. Martin & Mayer N. Zald, (eds.). *Social Welfare in Society*. New York: Columbia University Press, 1981, p. 511.

BIBLIOGRAPHY

Adams, P. & Freeman, G. On the Political Character of Social Service Work. *Social Service Review*, December 1979, pp. 560–572.

Agger, R., Goldrich, D. & Swanson B. *The Rulers and the Ruled: Political Power and Impotence in American Communities.* New York: John Wiley, 1964.

Aiken M. & Alford, R. Community Structure and Innovation: Public Housing, Urban Renewal and The War on Poverty, In Terry Clark (ed.). *Comparative Community Politics,* New York: Halsted Press, 1974.

Aiken, M. & Mott, P. (eds.). *The Structure of Community Power.* New York: Random House, 1970.

Anton, T., Larkey, P., Linton, T., Epstein, J., Fox, J. Townsend, N. & Zawacki, C. *Understanding the Fiscal Impact of General Revenue Sharing.* Ann Arbor, Mich.: Institute of Public Policy Studies, 1975.

Arne, R. *The End of the Swedish Model?* Stockholm, Sweden: The Swedish Institute, 1980.

Baker, E.M., Stevens, B.A., Schecter, S.L. & Wright, H.A., *Federal Grants, The National Interest and State Response: A Review of Theory and Research.* Philadelphia: Temple University, Center for the Study of Federalism, 1974, p. 28.

Banfield, E.C. *Political Influence*. New York: The Free Press, 1960.

Baugh, D.A. The Cost of Poor Relief in South-East England, 1790–1834. *The Economic History Review*, February 1975, pp. 50–68.

Bell, W. Analytic Tools that are Useful in Evaluating Social Welfare Programs. *Council on Social Work Education*, 1970, mimeo, p. 2.

Binstock, R.H. "A Policy Agenda on Aging for the 1980's," *National Journal Issues Book*, pp. 4–10.

Blumberg, P. *Inequality in an Age of Decline*. New York: Oxford University Press, 1980.

Boulding, K. The Boundaries Between Social Policy and Economic Policy. *Social Work*, January 1967, p. 7.

Brandelius, P., *Election Year '79: Taxes—One of the Main Issues in the 1979 Election*. Stockholm, Sweden: The Swedish Institute, 1979.

Bremner, R. *From the Depths: The Discovery of Poverty in the United States*. New York: New York University Press, 1960, p. 138.

Brieland, D. Use of Research-Measuring the Unmeasurable: An Essay Review *Social Work Research and Abstracts*, Winter 1981, pp. 40–43. A review of C.H. Weiss with M. Bucuvalas, *Social Science Research and Decision-Making*. New York: Columbia University Press, 1980.

Bureau of Labor Statistics, *Handbook of Labor Statistics*, 1931, published as Bulletin No. 541. Washington, D.C.: U.S. Government Printing Office, 1931, p. 479.

Buxbaum, C.B. Cost-Benefit Analysis: The Mystique Versus the Reality. *Social Service Review*, September 1, 1981, pp. 453–471.

City of Clinton vs. Cedar Rapids and Missouri River Railroad Company. 24 Iowa 455, 1868.

Clark, J. *The Rise of a New Federalism: Federal-State Cooperation in the United States*. New York: Columbia Press, 1938, p. 8.

Clark, T.N. *Community Power and Policy Outputs: A Review of Urban Research*. Beverly Hills, Cal.: Sage Publications, 1973.

Clark, T.N. *Community Structure and Decision-Making: Comparative Analyses*. Scranton, Pa: Chandler Publishing, 1968.

Clark, T.N. Community Structure, Decision-Making, Budget Expenditures, and Urban Renewal in 51 American Communities. *American Sociological Review*, August 1968, *33*, pp. 576–593.

Clark, T.N. Leadership in American Cities: Resources, Inter-changes and the Press. Unpublished manuscript, Chicago, June 1973.

Clark, T.N. & Ferguson, L.C. *City Money*. New York: Columbia University Press, 1983.

Cohen, W. The New Federalism: Theory, Practice, Problems. *National Journal*, special report, March 1973, p. 14.

Coll, B.D. *Perspectives in Public Welfare: A History*. Washington, D.C.: U.S. Government Printing Office, U.S. Department of Health, Education and Welfare, Social and Rehabilitation Service, Office of Research, Demonstrations and Training, Intramural Division, 1969, pp. 73–74.

Committee on Federal Grants-in-Aid, Council of State Governments, *Federal Grants-in-Aid*. Washington, D.C.: The Council of State Governments, 1949.

Congressional Globe (Thirty-Third Congress, 1st Session, May 3, 1854), pp. 1061–1063. Reprinted in S.P. Breckinridge, *Public Welfare Administration in the United States: Selected Documents*. Chicago: University of Chicago Press, 1938. Reprinted in F. Breul & A. Wade, *Readings in Social Welfare Policy*, University of Chicago, School of Social Service Administration, p. III-D1.

Conte, C. Analysts are Confident of Economic Health as the Decade Proceeds. *The Wall Street Journal*, September 14, 1981, p. 1.

Crain, R.L., Katz, E. & Rosenthal, D.B. The Politics of Community Conflict: The Fluoridation Decision. Indianapolis: Bobbs-Merrill, 1967; In B.T. Downes (Ed.). *Cities and Suburbs: Selected Readings in Local Politics and Public Policy*. Belmont, California: Wadsworth Publishing, 1971.

Cronin, J. Department of History, University of Wisconsin-Milwaukee, personal communication, November 1981.

Dahl, R.A. *Who Governs? Democracy Power in an American City*. New Haven: Yale University Press, 1961.

Dalphin, J. *The Persistence of Social Inequality In America*. Cambridge: Schenkman Publishing Co., 1981.

Davis, A.F. *Spearheads for Reform: The Social Settlements and the Progressive Movement 1890–1914*. New York: Oxford University Press, 1974.

de Schweinitz, K. *England's Road to Social Security*. New York: A.S. Barnes & Co. Inc., 1961, p. 17.

de Tocqueville, A. *Democracy in America*. R.D. Heffner (ed.). New York: Mentor Books, 1956.

Dexter, L.A. The Job of a Congressman. In I. Scharhansky (ed.). *Policy Analysis in Political Science*. Chicago: Markham Publishing Co., 1970, pp. 259–269.

Digby, A. The Labor Market and the Continuity of Social Policy After 1834: The Case of the Eastern Counties. *The Economic History Review*, February 1975, p. 71.

Dobelstein, A.W. *Politics, Economics, and Public Welfare*. Englewood Cliffs, NJ: Prentice-Hall, Inc., 1980, pp. 103–119.

Dumhoff, G.W. *Who Really Rules? New Haven and Community Power Reexamined*. New Brunswick: Transaction Books, 1978.

Dye, T.R. *Understanding Public Policy*. Englewood Cliffs, New Jersey: Prentice-Hall, Inc., 1972.

Form, W.H. & Rytina J. Ideological Beliefs on the Distribution of Power in the United States. *American Sociological Review*, 34, February, pp. 19–31.

Freeman, H. & Sherwood, C. *Social Research and Social Policy*. Englewood Cliffs, N.J.: Prentice-Hall, Inc. 1970.

Fried, M. with Fitgerald, E., Gleicher, P., Hartman, C. & Blose, J., Ippolito, C., Bentz, E., *The World of the Urban Working Class*. Cambridge, Mass.: Harvard University Press, 1973.

Freidman, M. *Capitalism and Freedom*. Chicago: University of Chicago Press, 1972.

Gallagher, J.J., Models for Policy Analysis: Child and Family Policy. In R. Haskins & J.J. Gallagher (eds.). *Models For Analysis of Social Policy: An Introduction*. Norwood, N.J.: Ablex Publishing Co., 1981, pp. 37–77.

Galper, J., The Speenhamland Scales: Political, Social, or Economic Disaster? *Social Service Review*, March 1970, pp. 54–62.

Garvin, C., Smith, A.D., Reid, W.J., *The Work Incentive Experience*. Montclair, NJ.: Allanheld, Osmun & Co., 1978.

Gilbert, N. & Specht, H., *Dimensions of Social Welfare Policy*. Englewood Cliffs, New Jersey: Prentice-Hall, Inc., 1974.

Gilbert, N. & Specht, H., *Dimensions of Social Welfare Policy*. Englewood (2nd ed.). Itasca, Ill.: F.E. Peacock Pub. Inc., 1981.

Gill, D., *Unraveling Social Policy: Theory, Analysis, and Political Action Towards Social Equality*. Cambridge: Schenkman Publishing Co., 1973.

Gilderson, A.J. & Marshall, E., *Social Benefits in Sweden*. Stockholm, Sweden: The Swedish Institute, 1973.

Gold, H. & Scarpitti, F.R. (eds.). *Combatting Social Problems: Techniques of Intervention*. New York: Holt, Rinehart & Winston, 1967, p. 2.

Goodwin, R., The Shape of American Politics. *Commentary*, June 1967, 5, p. 36.

Grodzins, M., Elazar, D.J. (ed.). *The American System: A New View of Government in the United States*. Chicago: Rand McNally, 1966, pp. 51–59.

Hagan, J.L., Whatever Happened to 43 Elizabeth I, c. 2? *Social Service Review*, March 1982, pp. 108–119.

Handel, G., *Social Welfare in Western Society*. New York: Random House, 1982.

Hawley, W.D. & Wirt, F.M. (eds.). Englewood Cliffs, NJ: Prentice-Hall, 1974.

Heckscher, G., What is the Purpose of Welfare? *Social Change in Sweden*, 1982, No. 25, p. 4.

Heffernan, W.J., *Introduction to Social Welfare Policy: Power, Scarcity, and Common Human Needs*. Itasca, Ill.: F.E. Peacock Pub. Inc., 1979.

Heller, W., Economic Rays of Hope. *The Wall Street Journal*, December 31, 1980.

Hibbard, M., The Crisis in Social Policy Planning. *Social Service Review*, December 1981, pp. 557–567.

Hirshorn, L., Social Policy and the Life Cycle: A Developmental Perspective. *Social Service Review*, September 1977, p. 437.

Hofstadter, R. *Social Darwinism in American Thought*. Boston: Beacon Press, 1944, 1955.

Hunter, F. *Community Power Structure: A Study of Decision Makers.* Chapel Hill, N.C.: University of North Carolina Press, 1953.

Hyman, H.H. The Value Systems of Different Classes: A Social Psychological Contribution to the Analysis of Stratification. In H.D. Stein & R.A. Cloward (eds.). *Social Perspectives on Behavior.* Glencoe: The Free Press, 1958, p. 330.

James, D. Materialistic Individualism and Ethnocentrism. In D. James *Poverty, Politics, and Change,* New Jersey: Prentice-Hall, Inc., 1972, pp. 22–39.

Johnson, C., Castleberry, H.P., Ogden, D.M. Jr. & Swanson, T., *American National Government,* (5th ed.). New York: Thomas Y. Crowell, 1960, p. 124.

Jordan, W.K. *Philanthropy in England 1480–1660: A Study of the Changing Pattern of English Social Aspirations.* New York: Russell Sage Foundation, 1959, pp. 55–56.

Kahn, A.J. The Function of Social Work in the Modern World. In A.J. Kahn. *Issues in American Social Work,* New York: Columbia University Press, 1959, p. 12.

Kahn, A.J. *Theory and Practice of Social Planning.* New York: Russell Sage Foundation, 1969.

Kammerman, S.B. & Kahn, A.J. *Social Services in the United States: Policies and Programs.* Philadelphia: Temple University Press, 1976.

Kerson, T.S., The Social Work Relationship: A Form of Gift Exchange. *Social Work,* July 1978, p. 326–327.

Key, V.O. *The Administration of Federal Grants to the States.* Chicago: Public Administration Service, 1937, p. 4.

Kohn, M. *Class and Conformity: A Study of Values.* Homewood, Ill.: The Dorsey Press, 1969, p. 189.

Laumann, E.O., Verbrugge, L.M. & Pappi, F.U. A Causal Modeling Approach to the Study of a Community Elite's Influence Structure. *American Sociological Review,* April 1974, *39,* 16–174.

Leonard, E.M. *The Early History of English Poor Law.* London: Frank Cass & Co., Ltd., 1965.

Levitan, S.A., Rein, M., Warwick, D. *Work and Welfare Go Together.* Baltimore, Md.: The Johns Hopkins Press, 1972.

Lewis, M. Social Policy Research: A Guide to Legal and Government Documents. *Social Service Review*, December, 1976, *50*, pp. 647–654.

Long, N. The Local Community as an Ecology of Games, *American Journal of Sociology*, 1958, *64*, pp. 251–61.

Longmate, N. *The Workhouse.* New York: St. Martin's Press, 1974, p. 14.

Lux, R.C. Assistant Professor, Scripture, Sacred Heart School of Theology, personal communication, March 1982.

Lyon, L. & Bonjean. C.M. "Community Power and Policy Outputs: The Routines of Local Politics," *Urban Affairs Quarterly* 17:1 Sept. 81, pp. 3–21.

Lyon, L., Felice, L.G., Perryman, M.R. & Parker, E.S. Community Power and Population Increase: An Empirical Test of the Growth Machine Model. *American Journal of Sociology*, May 1981, *86:6*, 1387–1400.

MacRae, D. Jr., & Haskins, R. Models for Policy Analysis. In R. Haskins & J.J. Gallagher. *Models for Analysis of Social Policy: An Introduction.* Norwood, N.J.: Ablex Publishing Co., 1981, pp. 1–35.

Magill, R.S. *Community Decision-Making for Social Welfare: Federalism, City Government, and the Poor.* New York: Human Services Press, 1979.

Magill, R.S. Federalism, Grants-In-Aid, and Social Welfare Policy. *Social Casework*, December 1976, pp. 626–636.

Magill, R.S. Who Decides Revenue Sharing Allocations? *Social Work*, July 1977, pp. 297–300.

Magill, R.S. & Clark, T.N. Community Power and Decision Making; Recent Research and its Policy Implications. *Social Service Review*, March 1975, 49, 33–45.

Marmor, T. *The Politics of Medicare.* Chicago: Aldine, 1973.

Marshall, T.H. Value Problems of Welfare-Capitalism. *Journal of Social Policy*, January 1972, pp. 15–32.

Martin, G.T., Social Welfare Trends in the United States, in Martin, G.T. & Zald, M.N. (eds.), *Social Welfare in Society.* New York: Columbia University Press, 1981, pp. 503–512.

Martin, R.C. *The Cities and the Federal System.* New York: Atherton Press, 1965.

McMilan A.W. & Bixby, A.K. Social Welfare Expenditures, Fiscal Year 1978, *Social Security Bulletin*, May 1980, *43*, pp. 3–17.

Meenahan, T.M., Washington, R. *Social Policy and Social Welfare: Structure and Applications.* New York: The Free Press, 1980, pp. 90–91.

Merton, R.H. Social Structure and Anomie. In: *Social Theory and Social Structure.* Glencoe, Ill.: The Free Press, 1957.

Miller, L.S. Determinants of the Welfare Effort: A Critique and Contribution, *Social Service Review*, March 1976, pp. 57–79.

The Milwaukee Journal. *Percentage of U.S. Non-Whites Grows.* 1981, p. 1.

The Milwaukee Journal. *Households Are Smaller in 1980,* May 26, 1981, p. 4.

Miringoff, M.L. The Impact of Population Policy Upon Social Welfare, *Social Service Review,* September, 1980, pp. 303–304.

Morlock, L.A. Business Interests, Countervailing Groups and the Balance of Influence in 91 Cities. In Hawley, W.D., & Wirt, F.M. (eds.). *The Search for Community Power,* (2nd ed.). Englewood Cliffs, N.J.: Prentice-Hall, 1974.

Moroney, R.M. Policy Analysis Within a Value Theoretical Framwork. In: R. Haskins & J.J. Gallagher. *Models for Analysis of Social Policy: An Introduction.* Norwood, N.J.: Ablex Publishing Co., 1981, pp. 94–97.

Moynihan, D.P. Policy vs. Program in the '70s. *The Public Interest,* Summer 1970, pp. 90–100.

Nathan, R.P. Statement on Revenue Sharing. Senate Subcommittee on Intergovernmental Relations, June 5, 1974, p. 4.

National Association of Social Workers. *Table 54. American Association of Social Workers (AASW) Membership, 1921–55; National Association of Social Workers (NASW) Membership, 1956–79.* Statistics on Demographic and Social Trends, Washington, D.C., 1980, p. 52.

National Association of Social Workers, *Table 14. Families Ranked by Total Money Income in Constant (1974) Dollars and By Race of Head, 1947–78,* Statistics on Demographic and Social Welfare Trends, Washington, D.C., 1980, p. 15.

National Association of Social Workers, *Table 50. Full-time Student Enrollment in Master's Degree Programs in Accredited Schools of Social Work and Number of Accredited Schools in the United States and Canada, Selected Years, 1929–79.*

National Association of Social Workers. *Table 10. Marriage and Divorce Rates, Selected years, 1900–78.* Statistics on Demographic and Social Welfare Trends. Washington, D.C., 1980. p. 12.

National Association of Social Workers. *Table 51. Students in Accredited Baccalaureate Social Work Programs, By Type of Enrollment, 1974–78.* Statistics on Demographic and Social Welfare Trends, Washington, D.C., 1980, p. 51.

Neuman, M. Speenhamland in Berkshire. In Martin (ed.). *Comparative Developments in Social Welfare,* pp. 85–127.

Niebuhr, R. *Moral Man and Immoral Society: A Study In Ethics and Politics.* New York, Charles Scribner, 1960.

Ohlin, L. & Cloward, R. *Delinquency and Opportunity.* Glencoe, Ill.: The Free Press, 1960.

Olds, V. The Freedmen's Bureau: A Nineteenth-Century Federal Welfare Agency. *Social Casework,* May 1963, *44,* 251–252.

Oxley, G.W. *Poor Relief for England and Wales 1601–1834.* London: David & Charles, 1974.

Perlman, R. & Gurin. A. *Community Organization and Social Planning.* New York: John Wiley & Sons, 1972.

Piven F.F. & Cloward, R. A. *Regulating the Poor: The Functions of Public Welfare.* New York: Pantheon Books, 1971.

Piven, F.F., & Cloward, R.A. Keeping Labor Lean and Hungry. *The Nation,* Nov. 7, 81, pp. 466–467.

Polanyi, K. *The Great Transformation.* Boston, Beacon Press, 1944.

Polsby, N.W. *Community Power and Political Theory: A Further Look at Problems of Evidence and Inference.* (2nd enlarged ed.). New Haven: Yale University Press, 1980.

Polsby, N.W. Empirical Investigation of the Mobilization of Bias in Community Power Research. *Political Studies,* December 1979, (Vol. 27:4) pp. 527–541.

Presthus, R. *Men at the Top: A Study of Community Power.* New York: Oxford University Press, 1964.

Prigmore, C.S. & Atherton, C.R. *Social Welfare Policy: Analysis and Formulation.* Lexington, Massachusetts: D.C. Heath & Company, 1979.

Pruger, R. Social Policy: Unilateral Transfer or Reciprocal Exchange. *Journal of Social Policy,* October 1973, pp. 289–302.

Rawls, J. *A Theory of Justice.* Cambridge, Mass.: Belknap Press, 1971.

Reagen, M.D. *The New Federalism.* New York: Oxford University Press, 1972, pp. 20–21.

Rein, M. Equality and Social Policy. *Social Service Review,* December 1977, pp. 565–587.

Rein, M. *Social Policy: Issues of Choice and Change.* New York: Random House, 1970.

Rein, M. Work in Welfare: Past Failures and Future Strategies. *Social Service Review,* June 1982, 211–229.

Resch, J.P. Federal Welfare for Revolutionary War Veterans. *Social Service Review,* June 1982, 171–195.

Rhoads, S.A. Economists and Policy Analysis. *Public Administration Review,* March, 1978, pp. 112–120.

Ricci, D. Receiving Ideas in Political Analysis: The Case of Community Power Studies: 1950–1970. *The Western Political Quarterly.* December 1980, 33:4, pp. 451–475.

Rimlinger, G. *Welfare Policy and Industrialization in Europe, America and Russia.* New York: John Wiley & Sons, 1971.

Rochefort, D.A. Progressive and Social Control Perspectives on Social Welfare, *Social Service Review,* December 1981, pp. 568–592.

Rossi, P.H., Berk, R.A. & Eidson, B.K. *The Roots of Urban Discontent.* New York: Wiley-Interscience, 1974.

Rothman, J. *Planning and Organizing for Social Change: Action Principles from Social Science Research.* New York: Columbia University Press, 1974, pp. 142–150.

Ryan, W. *Blaming the Victim.* New York: Pantheon Books, 1971.

Samuelson, P.A. *Economics* (9th ed.). New York: McGraw-Hill Book Company, 1973, p. 84.

Schenk, Q. with Schenk, E.L. *Welfare, Society, and the Helping Professions: An Introduction.* New York: Macmillan Publishing Co., Inc., 1981.

Schram, S.F. Politics, Professionalism, and the Changing Federalism *Social Service Review,* (March 1981, pp. 78–92.

Schick, A. Systems Politics and Systems Budgeting. *Public Administration Review,* March/April, 1969, pp. 137–151.

Schumaker, P.D., Getter, R.W., Clark, T.N. *Policy Responsiveness and Fiscal Strain in 51 American Communities.* Washington, D.C.: The American Political Science Association, 1979, pp. 20–21.

Sklar, M.H. The Impact of Revenue Sharing on Minorities and the Poor. *Harvard Civil Rights Civil Liberties Law Review,* January 1975, p. 103.

Smith, R. Poor Law and Poor Relief in the 19th Century Midlands. *Midland History,* (Vol. 2) 1974, No. 4, pp. 216–224.

Subcommittee on Intergovernmental Relations, Committee on Governmental Operation, U.S. Senate, *Creative Federalism,* 89th Congress, 2nd Session, 1966, Part I, p. 268.

Sundquist, J.L. *Politics and Policy: The Eisenhower, Kennedy, and Johnson Years.* Washington, D.C.: The Brookings Institution, 1968.

Sundquist, J.L. with the collaboration of Davis, D.W. *Making Federalism Work: A study of Program Coordination at the Community Level.* Washington, D.C.: The Brookings Institution, 1969, p. 1.

Taylor, J.S. The Unreformed Workhouse, 1776–1834. In: E.W. Martin (ed.). *Comparative Development in Social Welfare.* London: George Allen & Unwin Ltd., 1972, pp. 57–84.

Terrell, P. Adapting to Austerity: Human Services After Proposition 13. *Social Work,* July 1981, p. 275.

Thurow, L.C. *The Zero Sum Society: Distribution and the Possibilities for Economic Change.* New York: Basic Books, 1980.

Titmuss, R. *The Gift Relationship; From Human Blood to Social Policy.* New York: Pantheon Books, 1971.

Titmuss, R. The Limits of the Welfare State. *The Correspondent,* no. 31, March–April, 1964, p. 46.

Titmuss, R. The Role of Redistribution in Social Policy. *Social Security Bulletin,* June 1969, p. 1.

Trattner, W. *From Poor Law to Welfare State: A History of Social Welfare in America*. New York: The Free Press, 1979.

Tropman, J.E. The Constant Crisis: Social Welfare and the American Cultural Structure, *California Sociologist* 1978, 1(1), pp. 59–88.

Tropman, J.E. Societal Values and Social Policy: Implications for Social Work. In: G.T. Martin & Mayer Zald (eds.). *Social Welfare in Society*. New York: Columbia University Press, 1981, pp. 87–104.

Tyrmand, L. The Conservative Ideas in Reagan's Victory. *The Wall Street Journal*, January 20, 1981.

U.S. Bureau of the Census, *Statistical Abstract of the United States:* 1980 (101st ed.). Washington, D.C., 1980, p. 257.

United States Department of Labor, Bureau of Labor Statistics, News, *Earnings of Workers and Their Families; Fourth Quarter of 1980*. Washington, D.C., March 5, 1981.

Verba, S. & Nie, N.H. *Participation in America*. New York: Harper & Row, 1972.

Walton, J. The Bearing of Social Science Research on Public Issues: Floyd Hunter and the Study of Power. In: J. Walton & D.E. Carns., (eds.), *Cities in Change: Studies on the Urban Social Condition* (2nd ed.). Boston: Allyn & Bacon, 1977, pp. 263–272.

Warren, R. *The Community in America*. (2nd ed.). Chicago: Rand McNally, 1972.

Wheeler, G.R. The Social Welfare Consequences of General Revenue Sharing. *Public Welfare*, Summer 1972, p. 5.

Wilensky, H. & Lebeaux, C.N. *Industrial Society and Social Welfare*, New York: Russell Sage Foundation, 1958, p. 138.

Williams, A.S. Relationships Between the Structural Influence and Policy Outcomes. *Rural Sociology*, 1980, 45(4), pp. 621–643.

Wolk, J.L. Are Social Workers Politically Active? *Social Work*, July 1981, pp. 283–288.

Woodroofe, K. *From Charity to Social Work in England and the United States*. Toronto: University of Toronto Press, 1962.

Zald, M. Demographics, Politics, and the Future of the Welfare State. *Social Service Review*, March 1977.

Zweig, F. & Morris, R. The Social Planning Design Guide: Process and Proposal. *Social Work*, April 1966, pp. 13–21.

INDEX